THE NEW RETIREMENT STANDARD

JAMES WEISS, ChFC®, RICP® & **LOREN MERKLE,** CFP®

THE NEW RETIREMENT STANDARD

**POWERFUL PLANNING
TECHNIQUES TO LIVE FINANCIALLY FREE
IN RETIREMENT**

Published by Advantage, Charleston, South Carolina.
Member of Advantage Media Group.

ADVANTAGE is a registered trademark, and the Advantage colophon is a trademark of Advantage Media Group, Inc.

Printed in the United States of America.

ISBN: 978-1-59932-717-4
LCCN: 2016954299

Cover design by Megan Elger.

This publication is designed to provide accurate and authoritative information in regard to the subject matter covered. It is sold with the understanding that the publisher is not engaged in rendering legal, accounting, or other professional services. If legal advice or other expert assistance is required, the services of a competent professional person should be sought.

Advantage Media Group is proud to be a part of the Tree Neutral® program. Tree Neutral offsets the number of trees consumed in the production and printing of this book by taking proactive steps such as planting trees in direct proportion to the number of trees used to print books. To learn more about Tree Neutral, please visit **www.treeneutral.com.**

Advantage Media Group is a publisher of business, self-improvement, and professional development books. We help entrepreneurs, business leaders, and professionals share their Stories, Passion, and Knowledge to help others Learn & Grow. Do you have a manuscript or book idea that you would like us to consider for publishing? Please visit **advantagefamily.com** or call **1.866.775.1696.**

I would like to dedicate this book to my parents, Al and Jean Merkle. Their selflessness and dedication to their family is truly my inspiration.

—Loren

I am dedicating this book to my grandparents, Merle Daley and John Weiss, for planting the seeds of the entrepreneurial dream and of what might some day be possible when I was a child. The stories that were told long after their passing away have set my belief system for the passion that I have for owning my own business.

—James

TABLE OF CONTENTS

A FIFTEEN-DOLLAR LESSON

Loren Merkle, CERTIFIED FINANCIAL PLANNER™

When I was eight years old, I lost $15 of my allowance somewhere on the beaches or trails along the shores of Lake Michigan. You might say I was not a happy camper. And I confess that even now, more than thirty years later, I still find myself wondering where that wallet might be whenever my family revisits our longtime haunt on the Upper Peninsula.

I grew up out in the eastern Iowa countryside, with my two brothers and sister as my only playmates on the farmland that my parents rented. We did not have a lot of money, but we certainly were not lacking in love. We managed to take a vacation most years to the campground that my mom had known since childhood—the same spot where we all still gather most years. It was a ten-hour trip by pickup truck. We rode in the bed, sleeping on blankets amid the camping gear as Dad drove through the night.

My parents had implemented an allowance program when I was six years old, in which I would get five dollars per month if I completed my chores to their standard. My mom was the judge and kept a calendar on the kitchen wall where she would mark a big red circle around the days where I fell short of her expectations. She would deduct fifty cents for every red circle, so mathematically I could have ended up owing money at the end of the month. It never happened, but it was a distinct possibility.

The state campground felt like paradise. Our campsite was sandy, like the beach, and on the other side of a big hill was lovely Lake Michigan. We would play all day on an isolated two-mile stretch of beach, and at dinner time we would run through the trails as our parents prepared the meal.

When we arrived at the lake that year, my mom gave me $15 of the allowance money I had earned over the previous three months. It seemed like a fortune. She offered to hold on to it for me, but I wanted control of my assets. I opened the Velcro tab of my wallet, inserted the bills, and put it back in my pocket. The next day, after hours of playing on the beach and running through the woods, I returned to the campsite for dinner—and my wallet was gone.

I was heartbroken. I kept wishing that somehow I could change the course of events that had led to this. Why had I insisted on pocketing all my earnings? One of my brothers said that earlier in the day he had noticed my wallet hanging partly out of my pocket. I felt a flash of anger. Why hadn't he told me?

But none of that mattered now. I searched for my wallet for the rest of that vacation. I retraced those trails many times. I looked under leaves. I kicked clumps of sand. The next year, when we returned to the same campground, I kept looking every day.

To me, it wasn't just $15. It represented three months of hard work. I was a determined saver. I specifically remember one trip to McDonalds, where we had to buy our own meal. I didn't enjoy the lesson at the time, but now as a parent I see the genius in the exercise. The four of us kids were sitting in the backseat of the car, and I was the only one without a meal. I could not get myself to part with my hard-earned money for a culinary delight that I knew would exist for only about five minutes. Instead of indulging in an oh-so-tasty cheeseburger and fries, all I could think about was not letting go of the money that had taken me about two weeks of hard work to earn. I felt some regrets as my siblings munched their meals beside me on the backseat and the delightful aroma filled the car. They tease me about that incident to this day. I'm told that I begged for their leftovers.

What did I learn from those experiences and others like them? There were three distinct lessons:

- Earning money requires hard work.

- Saving money takes discipline and sacrifice.

- Losing money is heart-wrenching.

Today, as a retirement planner, I work with people who need to protect themselves against losing their wallets. They need to make sure that what they have earned over the years stays securely in their pocket. Their retirement savings represent a lifetime of hard work, and unless they take precautions, they could lose it. The days on their calendar are numbered, and the money has to last as long as they do.

Many are deeply concerned about that. The recession that struck in 2008 is still fresh in their minds, and they don't want to lose 40 percent in one year of what took them decades to accumulate. That's a real fear. Those who experienced such losses had a feeling in their gut that was similar to the way eight-year-old me felt long ago on a Lake Michigan beach. They wished they could do it over, but they knew they couldn't.

So now the question becomes: *How do we avoid making the same mistake again?*

Heading into retirement is a transition that often comes with great uncertainty. You are arranging to be unemployed for the rest of your life, and that's bound to bring some anxiety even when you plan it well. Big losses, however, certainly can be preventable with foresight and sensible strategies. You can protect and grow your money for a fulfilling retirement—and that, in large part, is what this book is about.

I still think about my wallet sometimes, but mostly in terms of how relatively small events can shape our attitudes toward money. Back then, money seemed to have a mystical quality to it. I saw it as something that my friends' families had but that my family did not. One of my friends in middle school, for example, would bring boxes of fruit snacks to school. They were delicious, and I was jealous. I recall wishing that I could afford such an expensive treat and that one day I would be able to buy as many fruit snacks as I could eat.

Early impressions can stay with people for a lifetime. Sometimes those attitudes are healthy, but other times they may get in the way. As people plan their finances for the rest of their lives, they need to think deeply about such matters. I know that my parents and my own life experiences have taught me that money reflects hard work and dedication and that it should be saved and nurtured—not for its own sake but for the sake of good things to come. To me, these coming good things include security and freedom for my family and myself. Plus, money affords me the opportunity to help my community.

My early fascination with money stayed with me as my parents and I worked together to pay my college tuition. Not long into my college years, my oldest brother was in a serious car accident. He survived, but he was never the same—and neither was I. The accident made me recognize a fundamental truth: tomorrow is never guaranteed. I had been intensely focused on what I would accomplish next, but after that I realized the importance of balance. We must live for today as well. We need money for now as well as for later. There are only so many days you can circle on the calendar before they are gone.

I became more social after that and developed more meaningful friendships. I saw that many of those friends lacked a basic understanding of how money works and how to build upon what you earn. One friend, however, who was a few years older than me, seemed particularly savvy. His childhood, like mine, had been far from affluent, and yet as a college senior he already had money to invest. I followed his example—and thus began the course of a career that I have pursued ever since. I have combined a passion for financial affairs, teaching, and a sincere desire to help people better their lives.

ALL THOSE MOVING PARTS

James Weiss, Chartered Financial Consultant®,
Retirement Income Certified Professional®

The cute little girl told me that the dandelion in the yard across the street was pretty, and that she would love to hold it in her hand. I wasn't allowed to cross the street by myself, which is a reasonable rule for a six-year-old. Still, eager to impress, I decided to take the risk. I raced across the street, plucked the dandelion, and quickly turned to return with the trophy for my lovely neighbor. Only I never made it. I wound up slipping on the curb, falling on my face, and severely slicing my eyelid.

On the way home from the hospital, my mother didn't yell at me. "There are reasons that we have rules, James," she said. She made me swear to never break the rules again, no matter how persuasive a girl might be. I had just wanted my playmate to be pleased, and even though Mom appreciated my desire to help others, this was far too much of a sacrifice.

I already had given my parents some trying moments. Once, when they couldn't find me at dinnertime, they eventually discovered me peering under the neighbor's car, watching him change the oil and asking if I could help. I was fascinated by the wrenches and the equipment and all those moving parts.

"You've got to be more careful, Jamie," Mom told me. "You can't be crawling under cars." I'm sure the neighbor had no idea that she had been looking for me, and he wouldn't have let me get near anything dangerous, but still there was a principle here; I needed to follow the safety rules. To me, however, it was just a matter of finding out how things worked together. I was a kid who was delighted by the details. After all, how can you help somebody if you don't have all the information?

It was a trait that stayed with me. When I was twelve, our videocassette recorder stopped working, so I disassembled it and figured out the problem, and soon we were watching movies again. I felt proud and so grown up. I always wanted to know what the adults were up to. I wanted to figure out how all those details fit into the whole. I paid rapt attention to things that go over most kids' heads—including a lot of talk about money, particularly after the death of my grandfather.

Grandpa Merle died young, during triple bypass surgery at age fifty-six, but I remember him well. He was successful in business and real estate, and he also had to own a new Cadillac car every couple of years. I remember my grandma's proud smile when Merle would show up in the driveway with a new car, and he would remind everyone that you have to take good care of new clients when you're showing homes to them. After his passing, I overheard conversations about whether Grandma Betty would be all right. "Will she have enough money? Did Merle make arrangements for her?" And it turned out he certainly had. I heard words like "trust" and "investments," and it was clear that my grandpa had made a plan. Thanks to his foresight, Grandma Betty lived comfortably to age ninety-one.

All of the moving parts in his plan fascinated me. I didn't have a clue what those words meant, but I gathered that money played a big role in the world of adults and that a good plan was key to success.

Meanwhile, I watched my own parents struggle financially when Dad lost his job. I knew that my grandmother had money, but my parents never asked her for help. I believe they wanted to show us kids the importance of making it on our own, through hard work. They instilled in us a strong work ethic. Even when Dad was without work, he was up daily at the crack of dawn. "If you want to stay up late and hoot with the owls," he told us, "you're going to have to be ready to get up and scream with the eagles in the morning."

I believe my family's struggles in those days shaped me and developed in me a purpose and passion for helping others to understand what money is all about. Today, I help people grow their wealth. But at the end of the day, it's not about how much you accumulate. It's about where you're going and how well you use what you have so that you can attain your goals in life. You need to rally your resources toward a desired result.

My brothers and I got plenty of love and support, but I recall all that talk and concern about money and whether there would be enough. It resonated with me. I could see the worry on my parents' faces, and I could feel the stress. *This must be something really important if it takes up so much of their time*, I thought, *and I need to figure it out and understand why it means so much*. I wanted to know how it all fit together.

I remember sitting with my brother Jeff along the trail by our school where we would ride our bikes and jump the dirt mounds. When we were tired of biking, we would sit back and talk about life as we knew it and as we imagined it might be. We would talk about what we wanted to do when we grew up. I said I would own my own business and be a success. That's what my grandpa had done, and that's what I would do. I would plan well, and I would make it.

When I graduated from high school, though, I was still confused about the direction I would take. My parents wondered if I might want to take up auto mechanics, since I had long shown that propensity for fixing things and attending to the details. I had never done well with writing and spelling, to the point where I doubted whether I was even college material. I would have been astounded at the thought that I would ever write a book—putting these words down now is an accomplishment that I never imagined I would attain.

And then I earned a scholarship. It was from Shaffer's Auto Body, a local shop, and it was designed for young people with an interest in marketing. And so I headed to Iowa State University as a marketing major. I didn't do so well. I just didn't feel a commitment to that field, but I did become determined to get a degree. At one point, I landed an internship with Pepsi and considered shifting my degree to food science. I soon tired of that as well.

I kept coming back to the concept that had intrigued me since I was little: "How does money really work?" That's when I decided to switch my major to finance. Because I had changed my major, I lost my scholarship and had to work full time while pursuing that degree. I made it through the rest of college with a laser focus and decided that I would start my career in the investment world.

My first job was with MetLife, which introduced me to a variety of products and investments, and it was there I obtained my securities licenses. Then I moved to Principal Financial Group in Des Moines, where my role was to consult with people on their 401(k) investments. That's where I met Loren, and we worked together there for a while. Eventually,

I was promoted to the role of helping other advisors develop comprehensive financial planning strategies.

I made a major decision to leave corporate America after the recession. It was 2009 and I figured that I had built up a lot of expertise along with my licensing and designations, and so I found myself in my basement, with a phone book and a laptop, ready to launch my own business. My aim was to educate people to help spare them the pain that so many had felt as their portfolios dwindled.

After a successful year, Loren and I decided to partner. We combined our areas of expertise to create Weiss-Merkle Financial, with the goal of helping people retire with confidence. A lot of planners who have designations such as ours require a prospective client to have many millions of dollars in investable assets. We feel that everybody in America deserves a comprehensive plan and that it's not so much about how much money you have as it is about making the most of your resources.

I have long since risen from the basement. Today, we have a 3,300-square-foot office in Johnston, Iowa, with plenty of space for educational events. We also host the *Weiss-Merkle Financial Show* each week from inside our office. During each thirty-minute show we share insights on how to avoid retirement mistakes and how to build a retirement plan to get you to and through retirement. We also teach college and adult educational classes in the Des Moines area. The goal of all of these efforts is the same: to help people put together all the moving parts of a comprehensive plan for financial peace of mind.

DECISIONS OF A LIFETIME

You hear it all the time, trumpeted by the so-called experts: Social Security is going broke, so take your benefit as soon as you can get it. The majority of people are claiming their Social Security benefits prior to full retirement age.

It's clear that people are influenced by a lot of misinformation about Social Security, and it leads them to make decisions that might not be proper for them. The hype about the impending demise of the system does not help. Retirees are unnecessarily giving up money. A major university study reported that $10 billion is being left on the table due to improper Social Security decisions.

In the classes that we teach, we often talk about making wise Social Security decisions, and people sometimes tell us afterward that we seem to believe that you should never take your benefits early. But that's not true. What we believe is that you should learn about your options so that you can make the best decision for you and your family. Perhaps that *does* mean taking the benefit at age sixty-two—but perhaps there are ways you can get a bigger bang for your buck.

FORWARD WITH CONFIDENCE

When older retirees meet us, they often tell us that they wish they had met us five or ten years earlier because they have learned what they didn't know then and have made some mistakes that they regret. Hindsight is twenty-twenty.

What most retirees want is confidence. A 2015 survey found that only 22 percent of workers felt truly confident that they would have enough money for a comfortable retirement.[1] That is higher, at least, than it was in the wake of the 2008 recession, when the confidence level was at record lows. The ebb and flow of the market have much to do with how good people feel about their future.

It need not be that way. A holistic approach to retirement planning can dispel those fears and build confidence that you will enjoy many fruitful years come what may in the economy. You can enjoy your retirement predicated on educated decisions based upon your particular circumstances.

The financial services industry focuses on products. The marketing is designed that way. A lot of money is spent to convince the public that it's all about finding the next best

---

1 Ebri.org, "The 2015 Retirement Confidence Survey: Having a Retirement Savings Plan a Key Factor in Americans' Retirement Confidence," Employee Benefit Research Institute (April 2015), https://www.ebri.org/publications/ib/index.cfm?fa=ibDisp&content_id=5513.

financial product or hot investment that promises a successful retirement. That couldn't be further from the truth. A successful retirement requires comprehensive, holistic planning. You need to build strategies that look at how you will be doing five, ten, or twenty years down the road.

People come to us with a wide variety of concerns, but we see some prevailing themes. They want to know whether they will outlive their money. They wonder what will happen to their money if they were to pass away tomorrow—will they be able to leave it to their loved ones or charities, or will Uncle Sam step in to claim nearly half of what they spent a lifetime accumulating? They are concerned about losing much of their wealth if they need long-term care. In short, they want to maximize their resources while protecting their nest egg.

Holistic planning identifies and addresses your particular concerns. It deals with them from the start, so that you head confidently into retirement, and it keeps track of your changing needs and desires as the years pass. You begin with assurance, and you proceed with assurance. You are moving from your days of accumulating money to your days of preserving it to last the rest of your lifetime—and that requires careful management of all your resources.

"I'M THINKING ABOUT RETIRING..."

We have found that our ideal clients are those who are within ten years of retirement or are already retired. Those are folks who tend to understand the value of putting together a comprehensive plan.

Often we get a call from someone in his or her late fifties, saying something like this: "I'm thinking about retiring. I have to figure out what to do with my 401(k), but I'm not sure how that's going to affect my pension and Social Security. What should I do? And I have a couple hundred thousand dollars in a savings account, and I'm wondering whether I should be investing it and taking more risk . . ."

Many of our clients are couples who have been married for thirty years. They have two or three children and some grandchildren. Most of them own a house, generally in the suburbs. Many have worked in middle management. We have teachers and IT professionals and a variety of others.

Our clients tend to be social, and they enjoy traveling—or at least that is their intention once they retire. They have a trusting nature. They love to share pictures and stories about their adventures, their grandchildren, and their activities. They look forward to the freedom to spend more time with family.

A ROAD MAP TO PROSPERITY

Many of our clients have one more thing in common when they come in to see us: they have not put much thought into comprehensive financial planning. In fact, most people think that their product—their 401(k), their IRA, their savings account—*is* their financial plan. Actually it's only one component of it.

We explain that a true financial plan is more like a road map to retirement. Without that map, they will have a much harder time getting there. And yet most people spend more time planning a vacation trip than their retirement journey. If they are going to France, they determine the best flight, ponder what to pack, and they decide where to stay, how to get around, and which sites to see. They don't just show up at the airport one day.

And yet that is the approach that people often take to retirement. Certainly, you should spend more time figuring out all the ramifications of retirement than you spend on all the details of a family vacation. There is much to consider. In the next thirty or forty unemployed years, how will you live without that paycheck? How do you make the most of your 401(k), and how much can you withdraw from it? Which is the best choice for the payout of your pension, if you have one? How does that choice relate to your Social Security

5

decision? How will the choices that you make today influence your lifestyle when you're eighty-five or ninety-five?

Clients tell us that they are unsure how much risk they are taking, and should be taking, with their money. How would another year like 2008 affect their overall portfolio? They don't really know. It's certainly a legitimate fear. If your retirement begins on the cusp of a terrible market and you are forced to withdraw income from a portfolio already pummeled by the economy, your hopes for an abundant lifestyle could be dashed unless you have carefully planned for such a contingency. We will take a closer look at that in chapter 5.

Other clients come to us full of confusion and misinformation. They have heard so many different stories, some true but many distorted. Some people worry about fees that lie hidden within their 401(k)s. Some have heard that a particular financial vehicle is good and another is bad, but they don't really know why or under what circumstances. It can be difficult to distill wisdom from the barrage of information.

This is not a book of advice on how to beat the Dow Jones Industrial Average or the Standard & Poor's 500. It's not for people determined to get double-digit returns year in and year out. That is not our purpose here. We are looking for a long-term relationship with our clients so that we get to know them and their goals, and then we can create a financial plan designed to meet those objectives. That means we need to decide up front whether we are a good fit for each other. If you just want us to beat an index, we are not for you.

Our planning process might not be a good approach for you if you are the type who likes to do it yourself and delve into the analytics, researching every stock and bond and exchange-traded fund (ETF). We have found that people with that kind of focus usually are mostly interested in chasing performance. They are more intent on finding the next best thing than the best long-term solutions. They are likely to feel frustrated by our strategic planning approach, which asks the hard questions and encourages some tough decisions. Instead of this book, they should be reading about financial market algorithms and high-frequency trading and the like.

Our book focuses on principles involved in transitioning confidently from your working life into retirement. You will be making crucial decisions involving your 401(k), Social Security, pension, savings, and much more, all of which will influence your comprehensive plan. You need to determine how each of those elements relates to the others and to your goals. This book is about *life planning*, and investment planning is but a part of it. Your investments need to fit your life. They should not define your life.

Many people experience a natural transition of mind-set as they approach the red zone of retirement, which is the ten years prior. Their attention turns to other things besides high-flying returns. They become far more attentive to how an economic slump might interfere with their plans and their desired lifestyle. They are concerned about running out of money before they run out of life. If that describes you, then keep turning these pages. We have written these words with you in mind.

CHAPTER 1

INTO A NEW WORLD

If you are like many people contemplating retirement, you have been accustomed to the world of work for decades, perhaps half a century. Your alarm goes off, you shower, and head out the door to be somewhere by a certain time, to perform certain functions, to meet certain standards.

And then it ends. You flip the retirement switch, and the next day you don't go back to your workplace. You have anticipated this day, perhaps longed for it, but it might not be quite what you expected. You could even feel a sense of loss. Often it takes months to adjust to the change of pace. Your body is still living by the alarm and the demands of the workaday world.

This lack of structure can feel alien. Some just can't let go, for a variety of reasons. One client who had been excited about retiring stayed on the job an additional two years out of a sense of dedication to his employer, who told him he just couldn't find a good replacement. He gradually transitioned from full-time to part-time and then cut the ties. Sometimes people delay retirement out of a fear of the unknown. And some just have not gathered sufficient resources. They continue working, or go back to work, out of necessity.

Many people tell us, though, that once they have positively adjusted to retirement, they didn't know how they ever found time to hold down a job. Well-adjusted retirees begin to fill their days with things they actually *want* to do instead of fulfilling some job description.

There are many ways to make the transition. You create your retirement. It shouldn't be merely something you accept passively. You can make your retirement what you want it to be. Younger people sometimes envision that retirement will be a time of sitting on the beach with a Corona and a lime. What many people find is that a sedentary lifestyle is not for them, at least not every day. They want to get out of bed and head out to face the world with a purpose. They actually feel a strong motivation to get back to the workplace. Sometimes it's because they rediscover their spouses for the first time in decades and need to balance the together time with additional activities outside of the house. Maybe they just feel the need to keep contributing. Some launch a new business or start a new career.

In short, retirement is a time of choices. Ideally, you can do what you want to do. If you get up in the morning and go to work, it's not because you have to make money to pay the bills. It's because you want to do something productive, creative, or innovative.

A NEW BATCH OF CONCERNS

Certainly your concerns are far different from the earlier chapters of your life. Back in those accumulation days, your focus may have been on finding a home to build a family. Your thoughts turned to acquiring a mortgage, but you may still have had student loans to pay off—and you were considering paying even more to further your education.

As you looked ahead, you started thinking in terms not just of months or years but of decades. Where would you be in twenty years? Would you be married with a family to support? You were becoming increasingly aware of the need to save for the long term, but life held so many distractions. You faced a lot of competing desires and worries. As the years passed, thoughts of retirement came to mind more frequently.

Now, as you prepare for that big step, you find that your worries are far different from what preoccupied that younger version of you. Instead of paying for your own schooling, or your children's, perhaps you have grandchildren whom you want to help. It's likely that you are starting to deal with health concerns. In almost every meeting with prospective new clients, we hear some heartfelt expression that reflects a deepening awareness of mortality. How would a spouse survive alone? How will they pay for mounting medical costs if their health fails? What if either or both spouses eventually need long-term care? And when the end does come, is there any way to stop Uncle Sam from laying claim to 40 or 50 percent of their life's work?

It's natural to think more about the value of time when you are older. It's in shorter supply. Younger people can ride the roller coaster of the markets with the knowledge that they won't need their investment money for decades. They can experience the plunges, knowing that before the ride is over they will soar high again. Older people tend to fear, with good reason, that once they take that plunge, they might not make it back up. It's just too steep a climb, and they don't have time. They tend to become more conservative with their investments.

For years, your perspective was: "How much can I save, and will it be enough?" As you approach retirement, your perspective becomes: "How much can I spend now and still have enough money for my whole retirement?" Retirees want to finally enjoy the resources that they sacrificed to attain. They want to know, as closely as possible, the rate at which they can spend without overdoing it.

We have worked with many people just like you, and we have seen a wide array of retirement scenarios. We do not get sidetracked on the concerns of those thirty- or forty-year-olds in the accumulation phase of their lives. We focus *solely*, day in and day out, on the concerns of those who are entering retirement or who already are there. That is why we are so knowledgeable, for example, about Social Security matters. We watch for changes in tax law that might affect our clients. We stay abreast of changing rules and regulations.

As the ranks of retirees swell, you can be sure that you are far from alone in the types of issues that you are facing. You will have your own particular set of circumstances, but themes of retirement planning tend to be similar. The key to a prosperous retirement is to recognize those themes and apply them to your unique needs and goals.

CHAPTER 2

DECIDING YOUR DESTINATION

When we sit down with new clients and ask them about their legacy ambitions, a husband and wife often will look at each other in silence. They clearly have never thought about it or discussed it. But now the wheels start to turn. Now we can engage in an open dialogue about where they would like their hard-earned resources to go someday.

That's a good place to start as they begin to work out a budget that will keep them on track toward their goals. We can work backward from the goals to determine what that budget should look like during retirement.

In our experience, only a few percent of people have a budget. Most cannot tell us what they anticipate needing, nor what they are currently spending each month. Without that knowledge, they have no idea how much they can spend in their retirement years. And so we show them a framework by which they can begin to track their spending.

Unless you know where you are going, however, how can you determine the amount of spending necessary to get there? That is why a crucial early step in our financial planning process is to help people figure out that destination. That quizzical look that we so often see on couple's faces tells us that they have been so caught up in the rush of life that they have yet to consider what it all means. Some have been intent on saving and some on spending, but they have not gotten around to talking about what they want out of life.

In short, they don't know. And when you don't know, you pay consequences. We have met couples who believe that they can do a whole lot more than their resources will support. We have met other couples of substantial means who live like paupers.

One hard-working couple who had pinched their pennies for years entered retirement with multiple millions of investable dollars. But when the paychecks stopped, they felt gripped by anxiety, concerned that they could run out of money—though it is highly unlikely that they would. Another couple who had what some would consider a marginal retirement account purchased a motor home with the intent of constantly traveling, without a care in the world that they might run out of money. It is highly likely that they *will*.

WEIGHING THE PRIORITIES

We have met people of many mind-sets when it comes to money. If they become clients, we help them to manage those mind-sets so that they can keep their ambitions and lifestyles aligned with their resources.

Most of those who become our clients acknowledge that they have long needed a comprehensive retirement plan, but they got busy raising kids and buying a house and developing their careers. They figured they would put their plan together when they got their next promotion or raise and had a few extra dollars, but that time came and went and came again, and the planning didn't happen. Perhaps they were waiting for some pivotal point in life that never arrived. Before they knew it, they were within a few years of retirement, and they still lacked a game plan.

Once they have concluded that it's high time to focus on their approaching retirement, we can get started in earnest. And the first step is establishing those goals and priorities. Again, you cannot plan until you know what you want to do.

When prospective clients are preparing to come in for their first meeting, they often ask us what they should bring. We tell them that if they have questions on some specific matter, they can bring those documents, but they do not need to do so.

That early conversation, in fact, often is best when you don't bring any documents or statements. We want to start out by focusing on you. We want to learn about you and your concerns and your dreams. We want to hear what you are trying to accomplish. At this point, we're not concerned about examining your portfolio. We want to know about *you*, not about your money.

There'll come a time and a place for the documents, but initially what is most important is that we connect with you and understand your concerns. We need to see if we would be a good fit in addressing those concerns, and we determine that by performing a three-pillar test:

1. Can we add value to your situation? If you are doing everything right, and we can't add value, then we will tell you so.

2. Is there good chemistry? James and I love meeting with clients. There needs to be good chemistry present or it won't work long term.

3. The relationship needs to be mutually beneficial. We learned a long time ago that we can't help everyone. Everyone needs to benefit from the relationship in order for it to be successful.

It's a matter of priorities. To get a grip on your priorities, we don't need to immediately see your tax returns and your holdings. Instead we need to look you in the eye and see what you are all about. We want to learn what you want out of life and why you felt the need to visit us. We talk about what keeps you up at night, and then we broaden the discussion to talk about how you might envision your retirement. What have you always wished you had time to do? Who and what are important to you? How do you believe you will find fulfillment? Is there someone you are hoping to help? Do you dream of traveling? Those are the sorts of questions that you could be considering.

Then we can start thinking about how much money you will need to accomplish those goals. The traditional advice is that during retirement you will need about 80 percent of the income that you brought in while working. Figuring that out can be quite complicated.

We take a different approach. What most people want to do is maintain the same lifestyle during retirement to which they have been accustomed. They want to continue spending about the same amount. Therefore, it makes sense to look at their budget and determine how much they actually have been spending.

We see two typical spending curves during retirement. One is during the first five or ten years, as people travel and play golf and pursue the hobbies that they had postponed. Eventually, the spending slows as they get a bit older and less active. That's the usual way of looking at changing spending needs during retirement. However, we increasingly have seen that expenses do not necessarily decrease with age. Instead, people begin to face expenses that they would rather avoid. Health-care costs inevitably rise, perhaps to the point of needing in-home nursing. They may need to spend money on things that are not fun to buy, such as shower tubs with walk in access or wheelchairs and ramps. The things you hope you would never need, however, they are a big expense later in life.

EXAMINING YOUR RESOURCES

After we get to know you and hear your dreams, then it's time to take a look at all the paperwork. We will want to examine the resources that you have available to meet the goals that you have described to us.

At that point, we give you a prepared list of information needed to design a financial plan for retirement. We will want to see your most recent Social Security statement, for example, which is now available online at SSA.gov. We will want a copy of your most recent tax return, including your W-2. We will be looking at any debts or liabilities, such as mortgages, car loans, or student loans, with associated payoff schedules and interest rates.

We will ask you to provide us with detailed investment statements so that we can see the ticker symbols of your securities. Your financial plan in part will include an investment analysis of how much risk you currently are taking and how much you are paying in fees, including hidden ones.

We also will be asking you to do some budgeting to determine how much you currently are spending and how much you anticipate you might need or want to spend during retirement. You should be thinking about what your retirement will look like so that we can begin designing a financial plan to make it happen.

Most people do not have all these documents at their fingertips. They are disorganized to some extent. That is another valuable benefit of our process. We assemble and file these documents so that you know where they are and your loved ones could access them easily in an emergency. That can save them untold hassles. Getting organized is a *loving* thing to do.

Your records will clearly indicate custodians of accounts; the dollar amounts, titling and beneficiaries of assets; and other estate documents such as trusts, a will, and powers of attorney. You can have all that at your fingertips. We encourage our clients to keep that information in a fireproof safe at home. Some people use a safety deposit box at the bank, but that can be challenging for beneficiaries to access.

Clients often have told us that this is the first time they ever have gathered all the documents in such a concise way in one spot. Often the information has become scattered over the years in various files in different desks. The financial plan also will include a one-page snapshot of all the accounts so that it will be easy to keep track.

How much of that information should you immediately share with your family or beneficiaries? It depends on family dynamics and personal preference. Some share all, some virtually nothing. At the very least, however, those who will be dealing with your affairs will need to know where your documents are kept and how to access them.

What is most important is to be prepared. Procrastination can be painful. An early step in our process is to do a beneficiary review. If we find any irregularities, those can easily be remedied while you are still alive, but when you are gone those beneficiary designations will be permanent. The consequences could be devastating. We want to make sure that your money goes where you want it to go.

Unfortunately, life can get in the way of effective planning. You need to force yourself to take the time out of your day to secure the rest of your life and to provide for those who will live after you. Once you have your financial plan in hand, you will be able to proceed with confidence.

Together, we serve as the head coach for the overall game plan. We are the dedicated resource for our clients and their heirs. They know they can reach out to us to find out where to start and how to finish. They know whom to contact about various issues and who will have which responsibilities. Your financial plan will be clear about who should be handling your financial affairs upon your passing.

Your financial plan needs to be more than a collection of products. It needs to be a strategy for getting from point A to point B. For thirty or forty years, you have tried to put away money to grow, but you might not have had an end strategy in mind. In the accumulation years, that worked for you. The gain was your aim. Now you need a strategy to connect the dots for the highest probability of a successful retirement. That begins with getting clear about just how you define success.

CHAPTER 3

A RETIREMENT REVOLUTION

Just a generation ago, retirement typically meant saying farewell to the coworkers you had known for decades and heading out with a generous pension provided by the good company to which you had hitched your cart most of your working life. On top of that, you switched on your Social Security benefits, and you were set. A comfortable middle-class lifestyle transitioned into a comfortable middle-class retirement.

The pension landscape has been changing dramatically. The golden age for pension plans was the 1960s and '70s and into the '80s. Today, few companies even offer pensions anymore, and recent legislation has allowed pension plans to discount even current retirees by up to 60 percent. Once, a solid pension could mean a happy and carefree retirement. Now, some of those retirees are heartbroken to see their benefits slashed. Some have been retired for a decade or more, and they no longer can count on those payments that had seemed so secure. The threshold is age eighty-five, beyond which your payments won't be cut unless the pension plan simply vanishes. If it happened to you, what would you do? Go back to work? Would anyone hire you at that age?

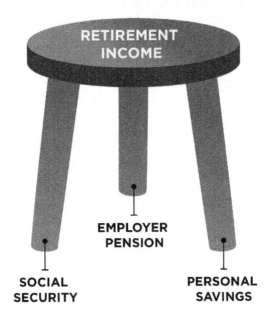

The traditional retirement model, often referred to as the "three-legged stool," includes three primary sources of income: your pension, your Social Security benefit, and whatever savings and investments you might have accumulated along the way. Clearly the nature of personal retirement planning needs to change if people are to live free of financial distress for what could be decades after their working days are over.

It's imperative to have a flexible plan that can change as life changes.

Unfortunately for many people--even those who have long depended on it-- the pension leg of that model is broken and could fall off. The Social Security leg is still in place, but many wonder what will become of it. Recent legislation will be eliminating the spousal benefit that many people had incorporated in their retirement planning. It will still be available for those born on or before January 1, 1954. For those born the next day or later, it's gone.

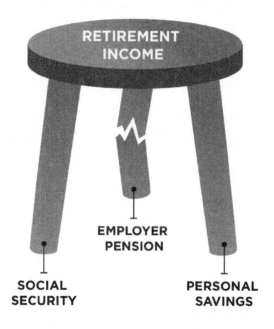

That leaves the third leg of the stool, the world of investments and savings, and it is now significantly different from what it was in the 1980s and earlier. In 1982, with interest rates topping at 18 percent, you could go down to the bank and get a certificate of deposit with a guaranteed return of 14 or 15 percent. Today, you would be lucky to get 1 percent on a CD. As retirees feel forced to turn to riskier investments with higher yields, the income stream is dicier. And so the third leg of the stool also has changed in a way that plays against the security of the retiree.

The country has seen a big shift—you could call it a revolution—in retirement planning since about 1974 with the advent of the Employee Retirement Income Security Act (ERISA). As companies increasingly turned to the new 401(k) s and away from the traditional pension plans, the responsibility shifted to the employees to make good investment decisions on their own behalf. Previously, the company bore the responsibility of taking care of its employees.

Over the years, however, it has become clear that many people have had a hard time understanding the type of investments they should include within their retirement plan. They do not have a grasp of how to create portfolios that will guarantee them income for the rest of their retirement. They do not know how to make the choices that will provide them with that type of certainty. It's a great concept to have more free choice in your investments, but along with that comes the responsibility of making prudent decisions and taking reasonable investment risks. That calls for knowledge of the three worlds of investing and how to use each with a portion of your money to maximize your resources. We'll explain that in detail in chapter 9.

THE SOCIAL SECURITY DECISION

When we ask people how they decided when to turn on their Social Security benefit, they often tell us that they got a letter a month before their sixty-second birthday saying they were entitled to perhaps $2,000 in monthly benefits. The letter led them to feel they needed to do something right away; otherwise, they would have to wait to age sixty-six or age seventy because those were the ages for which their antici-pated benefit was listed. They didn't realize that they could start their benefit at any point between. So they called the big 800 number on the letter, and a nice lady helped them set up direct deposits to their bank account. And that was how they made the Social Security decision. It took maybe fifteen minutes. It was as simple as that.

Let us assure you that it's *not* as simple as that!

Our approach to Social Security planning focuses instead on how the timing of when you elect to begin your benefits could really impact you. If you are entitled to, say, a present value of $2,000 a month in Social Security benefits, that can turn into a portfolio of $304,256 over the course of ten years. In twenty years, that could be $673,622, and in thirty years,

$1,160,479. That is how much is at stake in your fifteen-minute phone call.

That's why we put so much emphasis on helping people understand the importance of that decision. Most people don't think about the present value of those guaranteed income streams that will be available to them from the Social Security Administration. If you are in good health and your family has a history of longevity, you could easily live thirty years in retirement.

A thirty-year retirement once was unusual, but with advances in health care it's likely to be the norm for the coming wave of retirees. Their retirement could last longer than their working career. When the first regular, monthly Social Security check was paid in 1940, the average life expectancy for a male was sixty-one. Retirees could not claim a benefit until they were sixty-five. The system was designed so that a portion of the population would never collect any benefits, and those who did would likely only receive them for a few years. An actuarial study in the year 2000 determined that for a married couple age sixty-five, there was a 25 percent chance that one of them would live to age ninety-seven.[2] Think about how much technology has advanced since then—including medical science. Life expectancy is virtually certain to increase.

---

2 Robert J. Johansen, "Annuity 2000 Mortality Tables," Society of Actuaries, 2000.

These major changes call for different tools and strategies for retirement planning. The reason that we spend so much time educating our clients and people in the community about Social Security is to dispel the misinformation. Most people do not fully understand their options and rights. They risk making irrevocable decisions based on faulty information. Much of that misinformation comes from the media, but sometimes even Social Security workers get it wrong. Most are knowledgeable, but you might come across someone who is not—and the wrong decision could cost you tens of thousands of dollars throughout your retirement.

Nor will your advisor necessarily have all the information you need. Most advisors do not have an in-depth knowledge of Social Security. One reason for this is that retirement planning is not their specialty. Another is that they do not get a commission on your Social Security benefit. We are not concerned about the lack of commission on Social Security. That is not how we are compensated. We are concerned about doing the right thing and helping people to make the best decisions. You should be consulting with someone who understands your objectives and the complex nature of retirement planning. Social security planning is one of the more complicated elements of retirement planning to navigate.

Many people who elect to receive their Social Security benefits early explain that they have heard so much negativity in the news. They think of how much they paid into the system over the past thirty or thirty-five years, and they want to get some of it back while they can. They believe that the system is running out of money.

In reality, the Social Security trust fund is receiving more revenue today than ever. The baby boomers are in their peak wage-earning years, so more money is coming into the trust fund than it is paying out. It should remain that way until more of the boomers retire and start taking from the trust fund. Thus the Social Security system will be solvent for at least the next ten to fifteen years as of this 2016 writing.

So what's all the negativity about? Congress needs to review the trust fund solvency for the long-term, all the way out to the year 2085. It's true that somewhere between 2028 and 2033, the system faces the prospect of reducing everybody's payment by 25 percent unless Congress makes some changes.

There have been a variety of proposals, including the four-year phase-out of the spousal benefit strategies that commenced in 2016. And the retirement age might again be changed. Currently, some people will not be eligible for their full retirement age benefit until they are sixty-seven, and we believe that age will continually be moving up, particularly as life expectancy increases. Younger generations could see a retirement age of seventy or seventy-two.

We also might see smaller increases in cost-of-living adjustments, and the government might change the threshold at which wages are taxed. Currently, people are taxed on the first $118,500 that they earn. That limit could be set higher or eliminated so that all wages are taxed.

Those are among the measures that could be taken to maintain the solvency of the trust fund. We have a lot of flexibility. For the baby boomer demographic, the trust fund currently has enough to pay all benefits until at least the year 2028. Knowing that, you need not rush to turn on your benefits at age sixty-two, committing yourself to a smaller benefit for life. Instead you should have the confidence to be working on maximizing your resources.

Nonetheless, according to the Social Security Administration, only about 3 percent of people wait until after their full retirement age to claim benefits.[3] That is partly due to misuse of calculating tools that can be found online. Many financial advisors advocate them. One that often has been used is known as the break-even age calculator. The figures might show you that if you accepted a smaller benefit at age sixty-two instead of the larger one at full retirement age, it would take you until the age of seventy-eight to break even. Many prospective retirees figure they might as well get the

---

3 Melissa A. Z. Knoll and Anya Olsen, "Incentivizing Delayed Claiming of Social Security Retirement Benefits Before Reaching the Full Retirement Age," *Social Security Bulletin* 74, no. 4 (2014), https://www.ssa.gov/policy/docs/ssb/v74n4/v74n4p21.html.

money while they can because they would have to live sixteen years before they would have any additional benefit—and who's to say what will happen to the system by then?

For people who have never been married, the calculator can be a useful tool in guiding their decision. However, we caution people that if they *are* married, or once were, the break-even calculator will lead them to an improper decision more often than not. They have a wide variety of options on how they can elect to receive their benefit, and the calculator does not include all the survivorship and spousal benefits that are available. Instead, we advocate a more robust analysis that considers those options and provides accurate information for a better decision. We use a calculator that considers all eighty-one options, including the spousal and survivorship benefits, when conducting this analysis. A true Social Security analysis is customized to a couples' unique situation.

Many people do not understand how their benefit is derived. Your basic benefit is known as the "primary insurance amount." A critical component used to calculate the primary insurance amount is how much you earn during your working days.

The Social Security Administration calculates your earnings by looking at the highest thirty-five years of your wages. Those years need not be consecutive. Your benefit is based upon cherry picking your best years. If you had a few years of zero or low earnings—perhaps you took time off from your career to take care of the kids or were transitioning between jobs—those will not necessarily count against you if you had at least thirty-five other years of good earnings. Occasionally, however, a year also might be listed with zero earnings because your employer failed to report. That could significantly hurt your benefit. You should make sure that your earnings, as reported on page 3 of your Social Security statement, are correct and that the calculation is accurate. We have seen cases where the employer underreported earnings but never a case of overreporting.

The SSA indexes those best thirty-five years for inflation and then averages them to determine your benefit. You could very well be in a situation in which working a few more months beyond age sixty-two will get rid of one of your zeros and replace it with one of your higher wage-earning years. If doing so will add, say, $100 a month to your benefit, guaranteed throughout your retirement, that can be a big help in the long term.

Another component in determining the amount of your benefit is the age at which you elect to begin receiving it. If you turn it on as soon as you can, at age sixty-two, the system will apply a 25 percent actuarial reduction to your benefit. The penalty gets lower each year you get closer to your full retirement age.

Think of it this way: if your full retirement benefit is $2,000 a month but you choose to retire at sixty-two, you will be giving up about $260,000 over the course of the next thirty years. Why? Because $2,000 a month would have brought in a little over $1.1 million during that time, and you sacrificed a quarter of that by applying early.

Another crucial consideration if you are considering applying for an early benefit is whether you plan to continue working. The current earnings test is this: If you are under full retirement age, you will pay a penalty on any earnings over $15,720 a year. For every two dollars you make above that amount, you will lose one dollar of Social Security benefit. If you turn on your benefit at age sixty-two but after a year you realize it's not enough income and you need to go back to work, you must stay within the earnings limit or you will get hit with that penalty.

If this isn't already complex enough, the earned-income limit changes in the year that you reach full retirement age. The earnings limit moves to $41,880 for that year, and the penalty is decreased to a loss of $1 for every $3 you make over that limit. This restriction can significantly influence your decision on when to take your benefit.

Let's say your full retirement age is sixty-six and you reach that milestone on June 1, 2017. If you turn your benefit on prior to January 1, 2017, then you are restricted to earning only $15,720 for the year. Starting on January 1, 2017, you can make up to $3,490 per month and not be penalized. Once you turn sixty-six on June 1, the restriction vanishes and you can make as much as you want.

Tax ramifications are another issue that you must weigh if you're planning to continue working. Many people think that Social Security benefits are not taxable, whereas many states *do* tax them, and they also can be taxable at the federal level. For single people, a benefit amount that exceeds about $25,000 annually is currently considered to be taxable income. For married couples, the threshold is about $35,000. Up to 85 percent of your benefits can be taxed.

If you are willing to wait beyond your full retirement age to begin collecting your Social Security benefit, you can realize an additional gain. Many people do not know that they will get a guaranteed increase of about 8 percent for every year they hold off, up to age seventy. If you had a one-year CD that paid 8 percent, you probably would be quite impressed, considering that money sitting in the bank lately has been generating only about half a percent of interest.

As you plan your retirement strategy, it might make sense to spend down that money in the bank that is producing such a minuscule return so that you can take advantage of that annual increase in your Social Security benefit. In year one it's 8 percent; in year two, 16 percent; in year three, 24 percent;

and in year four, at age seventy, you will see a cumulative 32 percent increase in your benefit. That's quite a good return that you can get with a little planning.

"I wonder why my parents never talked about that," people often comment. It's because their parents did not have as much to gain. In 1982, interest rates were as high as 18 percent. Compared to that, the guaranteed 8 percent increase in Social Security benefit didn't matter much. In today's interest-rate environment, when rates have been next to zero, that annual boost in the benefit becomes much more attractive. It's a powerful tool that a lot of advisors do not advocate, because they do not understand how the system works.

Another advantage of the delaying strategy is that it could open up a four-year opportunity to convert some of your 401(k) or traditional IRA money (on which you would be required to pay taxes upon withdrawal at age seventy) into a tax-free Roth account. By delaying your benefit, you will not have that Social Security money coming into your tax bracket during those years, so you can accomplish the Roth conversion much more efficiently. Meanwhile, your benefit grows. We will take a closer look at such tax-saving strategies in chapter 6.

Though it might seem that we generally encourage people to delay taking their benefit, that is not the case. We are adamant about making sure that you pursue the strategy that is best for you. In fact, when we do an analysis for clients, the delay is often not the best course of action. What is most important is that you understand *all* the available options so that you can make the best decisions. If that means turning on your benefit at age sixty-two, then by all means do so. If it means waiting until age seventy, then that is what you should do. A lot of factors must be considered, and many of them are very personal ones. Just be sure that you are making an educated decision—not a spur-of-the-moment one based on a letter from the Social Security Administration and a brief call.

A CASE STUDY IN SOCIAL SECURITY

Let's look at the case of Mike and Mary, who are both at the full retirement age of sixty-six, which makes them eligible for the spousal benefit for people born before January 1, 1954. Mary's primary insurance amount is $800 a month. Mike's is $2,000 a month.

Mary files for her benefits to get her $800 a month. In doing so, she thereby enables Mike to apply for his spousal benefits. He is eligible for 50 percent of Mary's primary insurance or about $400 a month. Together they will be receiving $1,200 a month from Social Security for the next four years, until Mike is seventy. At that point, he switches over to his own benefit, which now has grown from $2,000 a month to $2,640 a month, thanks to the annual 8 percent boost. He will continue to get that for as long as he lives. Mary now is eligible to either continue receiving her own benefit or her spousal benefit, whichever is greater. She of course chooses her spousal benefit of $1,000.

This is what has happened: Mike and Mary got an extra $400 a month out of the system for four years, while Mike's benefit continued to grow in that time by a cumulative 32 percent. Now, at age seventy, they will be receiving $3,640 a month from Social Security for as long as both of them are alive. Let's say that Mike passes away two years later, at age seventy-two. Mary will then switch over to Mike's benefit because it's the highest. Therefore, she will continue to get $2,640 a month for the rest of her life.

That is a far more powerful strategy that produces much more income over their lifetimes than they would have received if Mike had filed for benefits at age sixty-two. Mary would not be receiving $2,640 a month as a widow. Instead, she would be receiving $1,500, the amount of Mike's reduced benefit.

Sometimes you just need to know the right questions to ask when you get that letter from the Social Security Administration. Mary likely would have been told about the $800 benefit to which she was entitled. She could have applied for that and been done with it. With an understanding of how the formula works, she was able to ask whether she could also apply for spousal benefits and increase their Social Security income as a couple. The Social Security representatives are not allowed to give you advice. They are there simply to answer your questions. If you don't ask them, you simply won't know. A knowledgeable advisor could ask those questions on your behalf, but unfortunately many advisors do not understand the nuances of the system.

CREATING YOUR OWN PENSION

The concern about maximizing your Social Security benefit illustrates how dramatically retirement planning has changed in the past generation. With pensions rapidly fading into insignificance, the other two legs of the stool—the Social Security benefit and your own investments—must fill the gap if you are to realize the retirement of your dreams.

In effect, you must create your own pension by rallying your own resources. In the chapters ahead, we will be taking a closer look at what is involved in doing so. Many people lack either the inclination, time, or skills to take care of their own investments—and there's nothing wrong with that, since we each have our own niche area of expertise. You may be brilliant at making money but need help with managing it. You should continue doing what you do best, and if that isn't money management, or if you are too busy, or if it just isn't your thing, then it's imperative that you find someone trustworthy with the skills and experience to do it on your behalf.

CHAPTER 4

THE RIGHT TEAM ON YOUR SIDE

During our first meeting with prospective clients, we give them the opportunity to broach any concerns that have been weighing on them as they approach retirement or as they adjust to it. Perhaps they have heard something around the water cooler that seems enticing or frightening, and they want a professional opinion. This is their chance to gauge not only our level of expertise but also whether we click with them in temperament and personality.

On our part, we are trying to determine whether they have grasped how important comprehensive planning is to a successful retirement. We have learned over the years that we simply are not a good fit for everyone. We cannot help everybody.

In one recent meeting with a couple, we asked, "So what are you hoping to accomplish today?" They shrugged and told us they just wanted to talk. Then we asked, "As you think about your retirement over the next five years, what concerns do you have?" They glanced at each other and then said, almost in unison, that they had no concerns.

That tells us one of two things: Either they haven't put much thought into their retirement and are not ready for the process, or all their issues already have been addressed. We cannot fix what is already fixed. We are looking to see whether prospective clients are serious about the process and whether we could be of service to them.

We are confident that once they get to know us, they will see that we have the expertise and pedigree to serve them well and that we are genuine and caring people. If that's what they need and want, that's what they will get—but if they are trying to accomplish something that does not fit our expertise, we will be up front about telling them that we are not a good match. Usually, that all becomes apparent in the course of our first meeting.

The goal is to help people identify what they need, where they are going, and what will work for them. Often, when people come to see us, we learn that something has been keeping them up at night. They face an issue that they do not know how to address. Generally, that's the first thing on the table. We want people to share those issues with us so that they will know right away whether their concern fits within our wheelhouse. If it does not, we certainly could refer them to somebody who might be more appropriate to help them. But if the issue is one of the many that we have dealt with numerous times, then we will explain how we can help and what the solution might look like.

We emphasize the need to get the right team on their side. We explain that we will work to produce a financial plan that will address their specific situation and reach for their goals in the months, years, and decades ahead.

A CUSTOMIZED APPROACH

A lot of people do not understand the difference between financial planners, such as us, and brokers who represent a company. After all, we dress similarly. And we list a lot of letters after our names. Most people, however, don't understand the significance of those designations and how they differentiate levels of expertise. People do not necessarily understand the true roles of those who present themselves as financial planners.

On the business card of a broker or representative, you typically will see the logo of the company or firm that they represent. Their primary role is to offer their in-house products that are available to the public. They are functioning as salespeople, trying to get customers to use their packaged products.

By contrast, think of the surgeon who is working with a team of others, each with an area of expertise and service. The surgeon depends upon the anesthesiologist and the nurses. They need one another. When it comes to financial planning, similar teamwork is necessary to do it right—and you get one shot to get your retirement right.

Together, we have three of the highest designations in our industry, CERTIFIED FINANCIAL PLANNER™ and Chartered Financial Consultant® and Retirement Income Certified Professional®. That is what qualifies us to put together comprehensive retirement plans and give advice holistically.

Americans are likely to enjoy a long retirement, and planning for that period is more complicated than ever before. Many don't have pensions to rely on the way their parents did and the strategy of living on fixed income investment earnings just doesn't work today. Complex and irrevocable decisions about when to retire, how to claim Social Security, and how to plan for the later years of retirement are required and interrelated. Mistakes in planning can mean running out of resources later in life when it's too late to do anything about it.

RICPs® work with clients like you to:

- Build a comprehensive retirement income plan that addresses income needs and other financial goals

- Choose your optimal retirement age

- Plan for the risks faced in retirement such as the uncertainties of life expectancy, inflation, health status, and investment climate

- Make claiming decisions that maximize Social Security benefits

- Obtain health insurance coverage to supplement Medicare or provide coverage prior to Medicare eligibility

- Plan for the consequences of frailty later in life including long-term care needs, and other needs due to physical and mental decline

- Consider ways to improve your plan through tax savings plans and other tax considerations

Retirees, and soon-to-be retirees like you, need to pick a well-trained, educated, and qualified financial professional to help develop their retirement income plan. When you find a CFP® or RICP®, you know that he or she has specific education and knowledge that can help you think through all the complexities of making your resources last throughout retirement.

We are not out to sell product off the shelf. If you meet an advisor who seems to want to sell you a product at your first meeting, that's a red flag that you are not dealing with a comprehensive planner. Instead, your initial conversations should be about your concerns and goals. What are you trying to accomplish?

Many of those who come to us have had experiences with other advisors, sometimes several, and a lot of those experiences have been bad. They do not necessarily recognize right away that what we will do for them is different than what those others did. It doesn't take long, however, for them to distinguish that our practice is structured quite differently than is typical in this industry.

Nobody wants to be sold. They want instead to be educated, particularly when it comes to something as important as their retirement. They want to hear about what is best for them, not what is best for the advisors. Virtually nobody who comes in to see us for the first time has a retirement plan. They usually have a pile of products that have been sold to them over the years without any clear direction or strategy on how that pile of products is going to properly position them for retirement.

You might say that we begin helping them clean out the closet. We will keep a pair of shoes and get rid of several others. We'll toss some shirts and get the wrinkles out of others. We rearrange the financial closet based on how they want to look in their retirement. We add a workable strategy to the products that makes sense as they strive to meet their goals.

We educate along the way, and our clients deeply appreciate that. We explain that they might accomplish their goals in many ways with a variety of products, and we provide recommendations and alternatives from which they can choose. We present the positives and the negatives and ask which ideas resonate and make the most sense to them. They need to feel good about what the plan will do for them. It's their choice, not ours.

If an advisor comes knocking at your door, you can reasonably presume that he or she is trying to sell you something. You will find a far different approach if you come into our office. Right off our main lobby is a learning center that shows our dedication to education for clients on a continuing basis. It's clear that people come back more than once to visit with us. One of our promises to families is that we will be there for their whole retirement and will keep them updated and educated on the many changes that are in store. Life will be changing, and we will be there for them when it does. We strive to create a family atmosphere and a long-term relationship.

We recognize that building a relationship means cultivating trust. Our industry has done much damage to trust through lack of transparency about the fees that people pay and how they pay them. Think of your experience when buying a car. Nobody is going to buy a car for the full retail price listed on the window. Instead, you determine a price that you would deem appropriate, and then you negotiate. However, in the investment world, people do pay the retail price for their investments—they just don't know it because of all the hidden fees attached to those products.

We believe that you should know exactly how much you are paying for what you are getting. You and your advisor need to sign off on it before any transaction takes place. That is how our practice is structured. You know what you are going to pay. You fully understand the services that you will be getting. That is the only way that you can adequately determine whether you are getting your money's worth. You would expect that from any business, and that is what you should be able to expect from the financial-services industry.

In this Internet-savvy world, some people have considered robo-advisors for their retirement planning. This has become a hot topic. Robo-advisors can be good at using fundamentals and technical analysis and algorithms to manage a portfolio. They can be powerful tools for people just starting out in retirement with limited resources. The technology could be helpful in the early management of a 401(k) or an IRA.

However, a robo-advisor typically will be good only at managing accounts that are at risk. But risk-based solutions are only one part of your retirement plan. You will also need money set aside as emergency savings, and you will need a portion of your money that is guaranteed. In other words, a sound retirement plan requires the customized and holistic approach, and a robo-advisor is not designed to deal with that.

If you are comfortable with the technology and have no qualms about taking advice through the Internet, a robo-advisor could be a good approach for a portion of your portfolio—but not all of it. You cannot take a cookie-cutter approach to your retirement planning and expect that you will be addressing all the concerns that will arise as life changes. Those algorithms can be helpful during the accumulation years, but they cannot account for your retirement dreams and your changing needs. There comes a time when only one-on-one human interaction will serve you well.

RISKY ADVICE

You should be wary as well about basing your retirement planning on what is served to you by the media. The media are highly self-serving instruments for disseminating information. Those twenty-four-hour news channels need to fill up airtime. They need to keep you watching and coming back. You wouldn't stay tuned if those commentators just told you everything was fine and no worries.

Inherently, the media go to the extremes. They try to evoke emotion. They present matters as worse than they might be—whatever it takes to get your attention. Unfortunately, people react emotionally to that type of information, and it often ends up hurting them. They take short-term maneuvers based on fear or greed, but in the long run they are worse off.

Consider, as well, who is spending the money to get that information out there. So much of the financial media coverage is about mutual funds, for example. You see them on the covers of magazines all the time: *this fund, that fund, look at what's hot!* You have to wonder why all those magazines put so much emphasis on what really is just one type of investment vehicle—and one in which people pay those full retail prices because they don't understand the hidden fees and costs. Who is paying for all that coverage?

Often we hear stories about people taking advice from friends and family and people at work. "My brother works in a large financial firm," someone will tell us, "and he says his 401(k) plan has been doing great and here's what I should be doing . . ." It turns out the brother works in the firm's IT department.

People are so desperate for information that they are willing to accept it at face value, regardless of the credibility of the source. Financial misinformation abounds, and people are susceptible to making improper decisions based upon it.

The Internet offers a vast amount of information, but where do you begin? How do you evaluate whether those sources are legitimate? How do you wade through it all? You can get information at the click of a button on almost any topic. If you run a search on virtually any investment vehicle, you will get countless hits. You will read about both the good and the bad. In truth, whether an investment or a financial product is good or bad depends on how you are using it. It depends upon you and your specific needs and goals.

Information comes easily. What is hard is to apply it with wisdom. None of those Internet wizards or media pundits knows anything about you. They know nothing about your situation or dreams. They, therefore, cannot possibly know whether any particular product will serve you well.

SUITABLE ISN'T SUFFICIENT

In our educational efforts, we explain the difference between a commission-based advisor, or what we call a representative, and an independent fiduciary advisor. The latter is how our firm is set up.

You can tell a lot from the disclosure at the bottom of a firm's business cards and the literature that it sends out. If the firm is offering securities through a broker-dealer arrangement, that typically means that the advisor is a representative of that firm. The company usually has proprietary products that they feel should be suitable for a client's situation.

Therein lies the big difference in our industry. Advisors who represent a firm mostly work in the *suitability* capacity, whereas Investment Advisor Representatives such as ourselves must maintain a *fiduciary* capacity. What does that mean? Let's say you are on a strict diet but ask a butcher what he might suggest. He no doubt will point to the chicken or pork or beef in the display cases, perhaps directing you to what is on sale. That is more or less what a non-fiduciary advisor will do—that is, offer you something out of the company's own bins. It will fill you up, for now, but you might suffer the consequences later.

If you really want to know what's best for you, though, you will consult with a dietitian who will consider your health needs and recommend precisely what will be good for you. You won't simply be sold whatever is available at the meat counter. You will have your choice of the healthiest ingredients throughout the entire store, and the dietitian will direct you to the proper aisles.

The dietitian is acting more in a fiduciary capacity. A fiduciary advisor must put your interests first and direct you to the products and decisions that make the most sense for what you are trying to accomplish. They must not simply be suitable. Sure, a particular product might be suitable for your situation. It also likely will be quite suitable for the advisor's situation. For example, investing $100,000 in a mutual fund with a 5 percent front-end commission might suit you. It certainly would please the advisor.

It's okay for advisors operating under the suitability standard to recommend a product that is not the best—just suitable. It might be an investment choice that would put you in the hole by $5,000 from the start because of tax consequences, but that's on you. The advisor isn't an accountant. Part of the reason you won't hear about such consequences is that the advisor simply doesn't know.

That's why those professional designations are critical when selecting someone to help you plan your retirement. You should be consulting with whichever is best able to help you. If you needed heart surgery, you wouldn't go to your general practitioner and say, "Okay, doc, open me up." You would go to a cardiologist with a support team of specialists. Unfortunately, in our industry, it's unlikely that an advisor with whom you have been working throughout your accumulation years will send you somewhere else for specialized care as you prepare to retire. Many advisors try to play both roles.

A lot of people dabble in financial planning. They get a securities license or an insurance license and do it part-time. You don't want them to be practicing on you. You only get one shot at retirement, and you need to do it right.

The advisor on your team should have a level of designation that clearly indicates dedication to higher education and particularly to financial planning. The kind of comprehensive planning that we do requires years to master the necessary skills. We have designations that you cannot obtain in just one exam. When choosing an advisor, look for a planning designation such as CFP® or ChFC®. If the advisor doesn't have a planning designation, then you know that person is in the product business, not the planning business.

QUALITIES OF A GOOD ADVISOR

It's always good to get at least three interviews with three advisors who have the appropriate planning designation. As a precaution, you might go to the website brokercheck.finra.org to see whether there has been any public discipline. And then trust your gut feelings. You might try to get the advisors you are interviewing outside their office environment. Perhaps you could take each of them to lunch. It might cost you $30, but the information that you gather will be well worth it. Are they polite to the waiter or waitress? Observe whether they treat others respectfully. You will learn much about how they likely would be treating you.

Above all, your advisor should be a good listener. In our industry there are a lot of type A personalities who like to talk a lot. They seem more interested in spouting out what is on their minds than finding out what is on *your* mind. You need an advisor who likes to listen and who knows the precise questions that will lead you to the right decisions. You need an advisor who can gather information, interpret it in a meaningful way, and use it in putting together your plan.

Pay attention to your gut feeling when you are talking to a prospective advisor. Does this person seem to genuinely care about you? Do you feel a rapport? Since so much depends upon the advisor's understanding of your specific situation, if you don't sense that depth of communication, something is wrong. The relationship is unlikely to be productive.

A good listener will be able to assimilate all your conversations over the course of several meetings and produce a document that will reassure you that you have been heard. You will see in writing what you have said you are trying to accomplish, your specific concerns, your timeline for retirement, and your projected spending. This will ensure that you both are on the same page. That is the nature of a true financial plan. It's not just some product that you have been sold.

In our planning process, we deliver what we call an income payout sheet. Let's say that you are sixty-two today, want to retire at sixty-six, and are spending $5,000 a month. We take into consideration your expected sources of income, including Social Security; figure in the inflation factor; and project the likely course of your retirement all the way to age one hundred. You can see that scenario on a single page. As one part of your plan to simplify all the different outputs and scenarios that we ran with the sub chapters of the comprehensive plan.

That's quite a contrast to the thirty- or forty-page document that many financial planners will produce with statistical data and algorithms that mean little to their clients because it's not a picture of their personal situation. It's just a collection of outputs and averages and past performances from financial instruments and tools. Amid the clutter, the clients cannot see much that encourages them to pursue their goals. We focus on providing the important information needed for critical decisions. We aim to empower, not overwhelm.

Think of yourself as the owner of the team, while we play the role of head coach. We work for you. Over the course of your retirement, we will be guiding you on a number of important decisions. Generally, there will be multiple ways that you could try to accomplish your goals. We narrow those down to a few that are most likely to work for you. We explain the positives and negatives and find out how you feel about them.

In short, we get to know each other very well. We are together through the ups and downs, the good and the bad, the joys and the sadness in life. We keep a box of tissues in our office because tears are not uncommon. Often the tears fall when a loved one has passed, but sometimes they come as a couple discusses, perhaps for the first time, issues that have been weighing heavily on their hearts. What was it all about? What was the purpose behind all of those years of working and saving? Sometimes we feel as if we are counselors as we witness such discussions unfold.

At times, when a couple is dealing with difficult issues, we have suggested that the whole family come in so that we can talk collectively about those concerns. When appropriate, we want the children to be fully aware of the decisions that might be coming up within a few years. Sometimes there is an elephant in the room. We help the family to see it. We help them to think through any issues rationally without letting emotions get in the way.

As you can see, what we do involves so much more than peddling product. We are dealing with human beings and family issues. And it's only when we understand the people that we can even begin to think about the right product to serve them.

CHAPTER 5

THREATS TO YOUR DOLLAR

Most people's thoughts turn to the stock market when they consider the financial risks that they could face. Certainly that is a major one. Many people have seen their fortunes fade when the market crashes. Others have sat on the sidelines, shell-shocked, as the market rebounds. Those fluctuations can make or break a portfolio, and human emotion has much to do with how well investors fare. They can be their own worst risk if they respond with fear or greed to the ebbs and flows of the market.

A major part of what we do for our clients is help them to recognize and manage risk—and those risks include much more than the prospect of tumbling securities. They face the threat of inflation, for example, and changing interest rates that can seriously erode their retirement income potential. They face the risk of paying too much in taxes and of losing ground to hidden fees within their investments. They run the risk that their portfolios simply will not be up to the task of lasting as long as they might live—and with medical advances, that is becoming an increasingly longer time. They risk the erosion of their life savings if the frailties of old age require long-term care.

All such risks must be considered in the preparation of a comprehensive financial plan for retirement because each can significantly impact the probability of success. Some of those risks—notably, taxes, fees, and long-term care—we will examine in upcoming chapters. Here, let's consider the others, starting with a closer look at the risk that most people think of first.

MARKET RISK

During your accumulation years it made little difference to you how the stock market performed in any particular year, so long as the trajectory over time was inevitably upward. If you were averaging a 7 percent rate of return, it didn't matter whether the good years came now or later. As long as you didn't take any money out of your account, the results would be the same.

That perspective changes dramatically in your retirement years. If you are withdrawing money for retirement income from a fluctuating account, and your portfolio takes a hit from the market, you will not have all those years ahead of you to recover as you did when you were younger. What's more, if those bad years come just as you are retiring, you may find it nearly impossible to regain what you lost. You still might average a 7 percent rate of return over the course of a decade in retirement, but now the sequence of returns will matter immensely. If the good years come early, your portfolio will be in far better shape.

Let's compare the performance of three sixty-five-year-old investors—we'll call them Jan, Bob, and Mike. Each has invested $1 million over twenty-five years, and each got the same 7 percent rate of return. Each of them also withdrew $60,000 every year, which, on the initial $1 million, was a 6 percent withdrawal rate.

The only difference was when the positive and negative years came within that investment period. For Jan, the first three years were very good ones. Mike got the same 7 percent return every year. Bob started out with two years of negative returns but then had three positive ones.

At the end of those twenty-five years, Jan had about $1.1 million. Mike ended up with $430,000. And Bob had nothing—he'd run out of money in the twenty-third year. That's a big disparity between the three portfolios, even though they all had the same average rate of return. The reason that Bob ran out of money was that the initial blow to his portfolio meant that the ensuing $60,000 withdrawals no longer represented 6 percent. To maintain that income, he was taking out a much higher percentage, and that had a dramatic immediate impact on the portfolio.

As you can see, it takes a lot to get back to even if you take a big hit, particularly when it's early in your retirement when you are withdrawing money. Most people don't understand the math. Let's say you have $100,000 and you lose 50 percent. Now you have a $50,000 portfolio. If you gain 50 percent the following year, how much will you have in your portfolio? Most people presume that they will be back to even at $100,000, but in reality you would have $75,000. After that initial 50 percent hit, it takes a full 100 percent rate of return just to get back to even. And that is presuming that you have withdrawn nothing from the account.

That is why people who lost half of their portfolio in 2008 struggled for so long to get back to even. The financial industry emphasizes averages when it markets investments, but those averages can be deceiving. The way that a security performed over five years, or ten years, has little bearing on how it performed within the specific conditions of your portfolio. The real performance of your investment is measured in how much you get to keep.

BALANCING YOUR PORTFOLIO

An essential discipline in dealing with market risk is to regularly rebalance your portfolio so that it remains aligned with the original level of risk that you determined you should be taking. You need to stay with your game plan.

A truly diversified portfolio will be composed of different asset classes, with an appropriate percentage of each. Once we establish our clients' goals for retirement, we can determine how much risk is necessary to accomplish them. We take into consideration their personal appetite for risk—how much can they tolerate? Then we invest accordingly.

Over time, however, adjustments will be necessary. Some asset classes and investments will perform much better than others for an extended period. That eventually will skew the risk percentages that we originally established. The winners will claim an ever-larger percentage of the portfolio unless we rebalance it.

Let's say that, in the past year, large companies performed much better than international companies. That means that the large-company allocation in your portfolio will be greater than we originally intended. To correct that, we need to take some of the investment out of the large companies and put it back into the international sector.

That accomplishes two things. It takes some profits (the ones that we gained from the large companies) off the table. That's a good move. And when we reinvest those into a depreciated asset class, we are buying more at a lower price. That, too, is a good move. As a result, we also have restored the original level of risk. Systematic rebalancing is a disciplined method of selling high and buying low, even when your emotions suggest you do otherwise.

Three decades ago, John Bogle, founder of the Vanguard Group, came up with the "Rule of 100," once a handy reference for do-it-yourself investors. According to the rule, you should subtract your age from one hundred, and the result is the percentage of your portfolio that you should expose to risk. The remainder should be in relatively conservative investments. In other words, the Rule of 100 suggests that you should regularly rebalance your portfolio as you get older so that it becomes increasingly less risky.

Today, however, investors have access to a much wider array of financial instruments. The rule was conceived before the Internet age, at a time when we lacked today's complex tools. There now are more types of investment vehicles than there are individual companies trading daily on the New York Stock Exchange. Such a simple rule no longer suffices.

We hesitate to give a thumbs-up to rules of thumb. They can lead you astray. Consider the current economic environment. Under the Rule of 100, if you are sixty-five years old today, you would have 65 percent of your assets invested in fixed or conservative instruments. However, consider the current interest and inflation rates. You might be getting 1 percent annually on a CD, while you are losing 2 percent in purchasing power. And if you are investing in bonds, take warning: when those low interest rates begin to increase, bond prices will decrease. You would lose money on your bond portfolio as well.

A rule of thumb might serve as a vague guide, but your plan tells us far more about how much risk you need to take—and whether you are on track toward your objectives.

INFLATION RISK

Inflation has always been with us. It's a risk that the individual investor cannot control, and it can sneak into a portfolio as a silent killer. We cannot make it go away, but we certainly can overcome it.

Most people pay little attention to inflation because it does its damage slowly over the years. You see no sudden and dramatic change, until one day you notice what has happened. It's like putting on weight—a pound here, five pounds there—until eventually you dislike what you see in the mirror and you find it harder to get around.

Inflation certainly can make it harder to get around. At a typical inflation rate of about 3 percent, a car that costs $50,000 today would cost more than $67,000 in ten years. In twenty years, it would cost $90,000-plus. It can be hard to grasp that reality, and so people tend to discount the real impact of inflation. Think back, though, to what you paid for your first new car. Was it $5,000 or perhaps $7,000? What would you be paying today?

Back in those days, you were probably getting regular promotions and pay raises as you were accumulating wealth. This kept your purchasing power on pace with inflation, and so you didn't think about it much. In retirement, once you no longer are receiving that salary, you need to create your own pay raises through the gain on your investments. Otherwise, as the years pass, you could see your objectives slipping out of reach.

INTEREST-RATE RISK

You also could be facing the distinct risk that future interest rates will cease to meet your expectations in providing retirement income. Let's say that you retired in 2006 and determined that your life savings needed to provide you with $50,000 of income a year. You had a $1 million portfolio, and back then it was not hard to get a 5 percent return on a guaranteed account. Your portfolio readily provided you with the income that you projected you would need. You were pleased that you did not need to dip into your principal.

Fast-forward to today. In the recent interest-rate environment, you might have been able to get a 1 percent return on that account. That means that the same million-dollar portfolio that generated $50,000 of income just a decade ago will now be generating only $10,000 of income.

That, in essence, is an illustration of interest-rate risk. As rates fluctuate, you face the prospect that you will no longer be able to obtain the rate on your portfolio that you had depended upon for your retirement lifestyle.

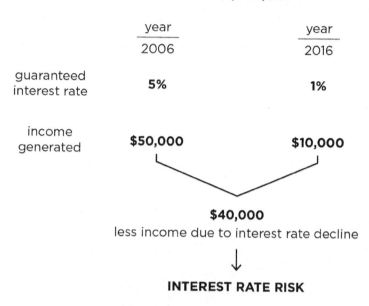

INTEREST RATE RISK

PORTFOLIO VALUE: $1,000,000

	year 2006	year 2016
guaranteed interest rate	5%	1%
income generated	$50,000	$10,000

$40,000
less income due to interest rate decline

↓

INTEREST RATE RISK

Your parents had a somewhat different experience with interest rates. Back in the early 1980s, interest rates were up to 18 or 19 percent. You could take your pot of money down to the bank and get a 14 percent guaranteed return. Meanwhile, inflation also was flying high. It might have seemed unimaginable to your parents that rates would ever fall as low as they have recently been. Basing a long-term retirement upon the rates of the moment is always risky business.

Interest-rate risk is of particular concern to bond investors. Imagine a teeter-totter, on which interest rates are at one end and bond values are at the other end. As the rates rise, the values fall. In general, that is the natural relationship between them. Interest rates recently have been not far above zero. Their side of the teeter-totter is down at the ground, and therefore the bond values on the other side are riding high. In today's environment, the purchase price of those bonds would be at a premium.

INTEREST RATES VS. BOND PRICES

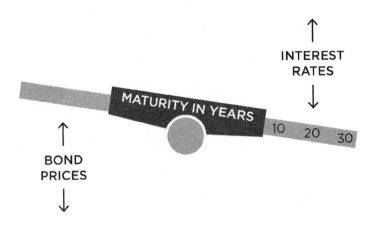

In other words, bond investors have recently been buying high. Rising interest rates might seem inevitable, considering that they could hardly go lower. When interest rates do rise, down come those bond values. It's important to understand that if you are allocating assets to what has long been considered a conservative investment in bonds, you could face an imminent risk of plunging prices. The idea is to buy low and sell high, not vice versa.

As you think about the risks that your portfolio faces during retirement, you can see that much of the threat is related to the fact that people are living so much longer. Retirement is likely to be far more than just a few years, and we must prepare for that potential.

The retirement years can be exciting and productive, but they come at a cost. We need a way to pay for all those extra years of living and loving and learning. Over the years, we also will feel the erosion of inflation unless we put it in its place. And longevity also brings with it inevitable health concerns, which will be among the additional risks that we will be exploring in upcoming chapters.

You can anticipate and manage most risks, even if you cannot fully control them. What is important is to take timely and informed action. One of the greatest risks could very well be human nature to procrastinate. People so often put off dealing with matters until they reach a crisis point, or they take action based on the fragility of their emotions, whether that is unbridled desire for more gain or an unreasonable fear of loss. You will do well to seek professional guidance in navigating your retirement years. That's an investment that should bring you great dividends.

ALL THAT GLITTERS . . .

Many people have been led to believe that they should be using gold within their portfolio as a hedge against threats to the dollar. The question often arises when it comes time to do an IRA or 401(k) rollover. In truth, gold is *not* an effective hedge.

Investing in gold dates to the days when the United States was printing dollars backed by the gold standard. In 1971, during the Nixon administration, the government removed the ability to convert dollars to gold. The goal was to let the market determine the dollar's value. Since then, it has been the market that has driven currencies.

If you wish to use gold in your IRA or qualified account, then you will need to have a custodian somewhere, and this arrangement can be expensive and confusing. You would get a paper statement showing you how many ounces of gold you own and the current price. If you own gold this way, the reality is that you don't really own anything more than a piece of paper. The real value of owning gold is the physical form you have at home in a safe. However, you can't hold physical gold in your safe and still get the benefits of an IRA or 401(k). It's usually not the best idea to roll over your 401(k) or IRA to gold because of these limitations that you have to hold gold inside a custodian instead of your own safe.

If, in some worst-case scenario, the dollar did collapse, think about how your gold investment would play out for you. Do you imagine that the custodian will be mailing you those gold coins in such a situation? Do you think that a UPS driver, if he knows he won't be getting a paycheck the following week, will be picking up the gold and bringing it to your house, even if it's certified mail?

The reality is that those things wouldn't happen in a worst-case scenario. The "hedge" of a gold position is actually just a way to make yourself feel better. It does not really protect your investment portfolio.

CHAPTER 6

MANAGING TAXES

Many people regard taxes as something that everyone just has to pay. They typically think that tax management and strategies involve taking advantage of some sort of loophole. Sometimes people worry that exercising the strategies could expose them to audit risk. That's far from the case. An audit is only a risk if you are breaking the tax law—and none of the strategies that we advocate will ever put our clients in the position of breaking laws.

In essence, tax management amounts to finding ways to apply the tax code to specific types of distributions and accounts. The tax code is thick and complex, with a multitude of options that taxpayers can use to maximize their resources. Those options were written into the code with the intent that people would apply them as needed. If they do not take those opportunities, they are at risk of handing over more to the government than they legally need to provide.

A major way that people engage in tax management is by taking advantage of the deferral potential available through 401(k) retirement plans and similar instruments. You get a tax deduction immediately for the money that you contribute, and it grows free of tax for all your working years until such time as you withdraw the money. However, the IRS remains a permanent partner in your plan. You will be required to begin withdrawing your money when you are age seventy and a half, whether you need it for income or not, and those required minimum distributions will be subjected to the prevailing tax rate in your bracket. If you have saved, say, $1 million and must withdraw $30,000, you will be taxed on it.

How much tax you pay will depend on whether you have anticipated those withdrawals in your tax management strategy. One option, if you are thinking a decade ahead, is to begin a strategy when you are sixty of converting money from your tax-deferred 401(k) plan into a tax-free Roth IRA. You can systematically pay taxes up front on those conversions over the ensuing decade. Gradually, a sizable portion of your portfolio will become tax-free for life.

The proper strategy will depend on your circumstances, of course. Much depends on whether you need the money as retirement income, or whether you would prefer to just leave it be, if you could.

TAX STATUS OF ACCOUNTS

From a tax perspective, there are three types of accounts: tax-deferred, tax-free, and taxable. Let's take a look at each.

The most common types of tax-deferred investments are 401(k) and similar plans, IRAs, and annuities in which you are not required to pay taxes on the gains every year. Eventually, when you pull that money out as income, you will have to pay the taxes then. Usually you will be paying at the ordinary income tax rate in your bracket.

Tax-free investments, by contrast, will provide you with distributions that are free of federal tax and sometimes free of state tax as well. The most common vehicle for tax-free investing is the Roth IRA, sometimes available as part of a 401(k) plan. Municipal bonds often are federally tax-free, as well. Life insurance also could be considered a tax-free investment, and certain educational accounts provide tax-free benefits.

Taxable investments are those that are subject to taxation in the year in which you realize the income, dividends, and capital gains. The most common types are individual equities and mutual funds, ETFs, individual bonds and bond funds, certificates of deposit, savings accounts, and money market accounts. Those have no tax-deferred or tax-free umbrella. You get no tax deduction on the money that you place in these investments, and you must pay taxes on them annually.

Effective financial planning for retirement will ensure that a portion of your assets is in each of those three tax categories. You might think of them as buckets, each for a different purpose. When you are younger, the use of tax-free and tax-deferred investments can provide you with compounding advantages that can significantly boost your portfolio by the time you are ready to retire. For example, in a taxable investment, you might save $3,000 a year for thirty years with 8 percent growth, but after paying taxes in the 28 percent bracket you would only have $173,000. Your money would not even have doubled in three decades. In a tax-free investment, like a Roth IRA, you would have $368,000 free and clear. That's also how much a tax-deferred investment, Like a 401(k) or IRA, would bring to you, except you would have a permanent partner in Uncle Sam who would eventually want his cut.

When you retire and you need to deliver an income to support your lifestyle, investments in all three buckets will provide you with a combination of assets that you can tap as needed, while making sure that your income remains in the lower brackets. Each bucket has distinct and powerful advantages, as well as some disadvantages. It takes the right balance and an educated management approach to make sure that you are not overpaying in taxes.

TAX STATUS OF ACCOUNTS

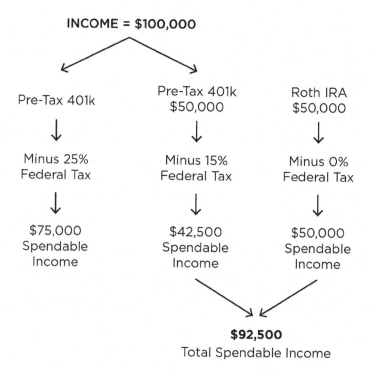

INCOME = $100,000

Pre-Tax 401k	Pre-Tax 401k $50,000	Roth IRA $50,000
↓	↓	↓
Minus 25% Federal Tax	Minus 15% Federal Tax	Minus 0% Federal Tax
↓	↓	↓
$75,000 Spendable Income	$42,500 Spendable Income	$50,000 Spendable Income

$92,500
Total Spendable Income

Tax-free and tax-deferred compounding can be a powerful tool for accumulating wealth during your working years, but you will need to be making adjustments as you enter retirement. Many people at that point have most or all of their money in just one bucket, the tax-deferred 401(k) plan.

Let's say you need $100,000 of income during retirement. If your only source is your 401(k), and you withdraw that much, you will be squarely in the 25 percent federal tax bracket if you file your taxes Married Filing Jointly. That means you will have spendable income of $75,000, with the balance going to Uncle Sam. However, let's say you did a little more planning and had money in just two of those three buckets, the tax-deferred one and the tax-free one. If you were to take $50,000 from each of those accounts, you would only be taxed on the $50,000 from the tax-deferred account. That would keep you in the 15 percent federal tax bracket. In other words, you have still withdrawn $100,000, but now you get to keep $92,500. Uncle Sam only gets $7,500, not $25,000.

It will take you some time to accumulate meaningful dollars for a strategy such as this, but it can be well worth the effort. You will have much more flexibility in designing your retirement income if you have done some sound planning in advance.

Often, when we talk to people about this type of tax-saving strategy, they regret that they have not funded a Roth account and wonder whether they have any options. It's not as if the Roth has been around for ages. It came about as a result of the Taxpayer Relief Act of 1997. Investors have not had decades to take advantage of it. And the Roth 401(k) plans have only been a phenomenon of the last several years. Not everybody has access to a Roth 401(k), and the Roth IRA has income limits, so not everybody can contribute to one.

"I'm too old for a Roth IRA," people sometimes tell us, or "it doesn't make sense for me to have a Roth IRA now, because I'm already in retirement." That is not necessarily the case at all. We can pursue a strategy that amounts to filling up your tax bracket. Let's say that you are a married couple filing jointly, which means that you will be in the 15 percent federal tax bracket up to the point where you have $75,000 of income. If your taxable income shortly after retirement is only $50,000, that means we have the potential for a $25,000 Roth conversion. You can accomplish that conversion and pay only a 15 percent tax hit. The next year you can do it again, converting just enough to keep you within that tax bracket.

The recent federal tax environment has been at historic lows. If we project five or ten years forward, it's likely (although not certain) that we will be seeing higher tax brackets. This strategy allows you to lock in your tax rate at 15 percent on the money that you are converting to a Roth. This will build up your tax-free assets so that later in retirement you can choose the bucket from which you will make withdrawals as a means of continuing to manage your tax bracket.

Those are just a few of the tax-saving strategies that you might implement, depending upon what you are trying to accomplish and the resources that are available to you. Another little-known strategy involves the "step-up" of cost basis upon death. The cost basis of certain assets will be reset to their current value when left to survivors, meaning the assets no longer will show a gain from their original value, and the survivors will not have to pay a capital-gains tax. In other words, if my mom had $100,000 in a nonqualified investment but she only originally invested $50,000 and she died, there would be a step up in cost basis to the full $100,000 for me. Therefore, I would only be responsible for tax on any gain over $100,000. If she spent the $100,000 while she was alive then she would be taxed on the difference between the $100,000 and the $50,000 original investment.

Couples sometimes will tell us that they are concerned about leaving a tax burden to their children when they pass away. They don't so much mind paying some tax on their current income, but they do not want to leave a burden on their estate. The step-up strategy in such cases can be quite useful.

Let's say a couple owns a significant amount of individual equities that have enjoyed quite a bit of appreciation. Instead of selling them off for income and paying tax on the gain, they could leave those securities to their children, who upon the parents' passing would get a 100 percent step-up in cost basis. If the couple has $500,000 worth of individual equities with a cost basis of $250,000 and sold those equities while they were alive, the couple would be paying a capital gains tax on the other $250,000 of growth. Their survivors, however, would "step up" that cost basis, so they would owe nothing in capital gains at the time they receive the money. That can be a valuable strategy for families with assets that qualify.

PHANTOM TAXES

We recently met a couple who had $3 million invested in taxable mutual funds, outside of a tax-deferred retirement plan. The account was providing them a valuable opportunity for growth, but it also was putting out income that they did not need. They were paying about $50,000 a year in taxes on capital gains.

Part of that was due to the phenomenon of "phantom tax" that is often seen with mutual funds. Let's say you purchased XYZ mutual fund in December. Well, that mutual fund has been buying and selling throughout the course of the year, realizing capital gains many times and certainly producing dividends within the portfolio. As part owner of that fund, you are liable at year's end for the tax that it has incurred during the entire year—even though you have been invested in it for only one month.

If you buy into the mutual fund on December 1 and it drops in value over the next thirty days, you actually could lose money on your investment but still be responsible for the year long gains within that fund. A lot of people do not understand how that works. They cannot conceive of how they could lose money on their investment but still owe tax based on its performance. Mutual funds, from a tax standpoint, can be very inefficient when not part of a tax-deferred portfolio such as a 401(k).

We helped that couple by selling and moving a portion of their money into a low-cost deferred annuity. In the process, we did some "tax harvesting," in which we offset gains on some investments with the losses on others. In the annuity, the money now had the potential for growth, but the couple no longer had to pay taxes on that growth. That significantly decreased their end-of-the-year tax bill and eliminated the phantom tax on that portion of their money.

STRETCH PROVISIONS

In our experience, we have found that the vast majority of all IRAs are liquidated upon the death of the surviving spouse. One reason for that is improper titling, as we pointed out earlier. The second most common reason is improper execution of the distribution.

Many people are unfamiliar with what are known as stretch provisions, which are available on accounts that are properly titled. All IRAs offer the stretch provision, but only some 401(k)s offer it. It depends upon the policy of the particular plan.

The stretch provision allows the beneficiary of the account to stretch out distributions over his or her lifetime. What happens most of the time, however, is that once the surviving spouse has passed away, the survivors simply liquidate what is left of the account. They take it as a lump sum, and that puts them in the highest tax bracket—meaning they will lose about 45 percent of it to the state and federal governments.

Alternatively survivors could take that distribution slowly over the course of their lifetime. That would keep them, potentially, in a much lower tax bracket while the asset continued to grow throughout those years. That stretch provision, however, needs to be set up in advance. If the distribution strategy is not appropriately executed, it simply won't happen. In order for this to work, the owner of the account needs to title it and set it up, and the beneficiary needs to execute on it. The beneficiary can take advantage of the full stretch, part of it, or none of it. He or she still can choose to take the lump sum, but at least a far more efficient tax strategy was available.

Unfortunately, young people inheriting a sum of money tend to find some immediate use for it. Perhaps they are facing financial difficulties or want to get out from under a debt or credit card bills, or perhaps they cannot resist the allure of a fancy sports car. That, no doubt, is why we have that statistic showing the survivors liquidate the account 90 percent of the time. They either don't know about the stretch provision, don't care about it, or have some pressing need for the money.

It's unfortunate. If stretched over another generation a relatively modest IRA could become a tidy sum. If left untouched for healthy growth, it could turn into a fortune. A couple with two children and two grandchildren, could turn a $525,000 IRA into a $4.5 million family legacy over the course of their lives. And that's all by appropriate titling and distribution execution on those accounts. So many people work hard to accumulate a nest egg and then do not understand the steps they need to take to properly title their assets. The consequences can be far from what they intended.

Even though you cannot enforce a stretch provision, you have another option. You can set up a trust so that your children do not have the ability to take the lump sum and make those common financial mistakes. If your twenty-four-year-old child inherits $500,000 all at once, it's hard for him or her to take a disciplined approach to managing it. He or she is unlikely to see the long-term value of accepting required minimum distributions each year. That is why some couples want to institute control mechanisms in the distribution of their money.

Through the use of a trust, it's possible to require the stretch rather than simply recommend it. You must be careful, however, when incorporating a trust as the beneficiary of an IRA. Very specific provisions must be written in the trust to allow the stretch. Most trusts that we review do not have the appropriate language to provide for that. After the IRA is deposited into the trust, the trust ordinarily has five years to liquidate it, and it then has to be taxed. The stretch provision therefore will disappear unless the trust is written appropriately to allow it. Generally, the trust should not be the primary beneficiary of an IRA. It makes sense only in rare circumstances. In any case, the language to incorporate the stretch provision must be written in a specific manner.

TAX STRATEGIES FOR SUCCESS

The complexity of the tax code is both an advantage and a disadvantage. It can be a disadvantage when the language becomes confusing and complicated. But if you understand the tax code, it can be highly advantageous. If you are willing to plan and work with someone who can help you interpret the details, you can implement strategies that could save you significant money on taxation in retirement.

In this chapter, we have touched on a few of those strategies. There are many others. The ones you choose will depend upon your particular situation and what you are trying to accomplish, and they will depend upon the resources at your disposal.

From a historical perspective, we have been in a low-tax era. In 1964, the highest marginal tax bracket was over 90 percent. As recently as the 1970s, the highest bracket was 70 percent. It seems reasonable to project that the recent low rates likely will be rising closer to the historic norm, particularly considering the levels of government debt that we are facing. With that in mind, it makes sense to take whatever measures are available now to lock in the lower rates and save on taxes down the road. Such strategies can go far toward improving the probability of an overall successful retirement.

HISTORICAL MARGINAL TAX RATE FOR HIGHEST AND LOWEST WAGE EARNERS

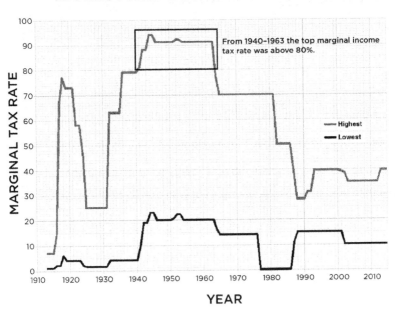

CHAPTER 7

BEWARE THE FEES

As fiduciaries, it's our duty to be transparent about the fees that we assess and that our clients pay. Such transparency often is lacking in our industry. One of the reasons that we do not advocate the use of mutual funds is their lack of transparency about the variety of fees charged within them.

Layers of hidden expenses lie inside the typical mutual fund. A 2011 study conducted by Forbes found that the average mutual fund costs in a taxable account totaled 4.17 percent per year. In nontaxable accounts, the industry average was 3.17 percent.

Compare those figures to the average expense ratio proclaimed in a mutual fund prospectus, which is 0.9 percent. As you can see, there is a major disparity between what the prospectus tells you that you are paying and what you are actually paying.

There are five main types of hidden costs associated with mutual funds, but let us focus here on some that people rarely know about.

Transaction cost: A big attraction of mutual fund investing is that you do not need to research individual securities and decide, for example, whether to buy IBM or sell AT&T. A professional management team does that for you. What may not be clear to you is that the buying and selling produce expenses that the managers pass on to you. They do not have to tell you what those costs are, however. The plan prospectus explains that the transactions produce commissions and that those commissions are not reported in the total annual operating expense. Those transaction expenses are the number-one hidden cost in most mutual funds. The Forbes study found that the average transactional cost in funds is 1.44 percent.

Cash drag: Because mutual funds are pooled investments in which millions of people participate, some of those investors on any given day will be liquidating all or a portion of their portfolios. The mutual fund must honor those liquidations, so it keeps cash on hand for the payouts. What does that mean to you? The fees that you pay are based upon 100 percent of the account value—including the portion that is sitting in cash doing nothing for you. This is what is known as cash drag, and it's a hidden expense that you will not find in a prospectus. The Forbes study found that the average cash drag expense in mutual funds is 0.83 percent. For every dollar you invest, you are losing nearly a penny to cash drag, each and every year. It adds up, particularly over the course of thirty or forty years.

Tax cost: One Forbes study estimated tax costs, on average, to be 1 to 2 percent.[4] These results are from the phantom tax on mutual funds, as I explained earlier. You might have owned a fund only for a month, but you end up paying taxes on it as if you have owned it for the entire year. Or perhaps you did own it for a year, but you discover that on December 31 the fund is worth less than when you bought it on January 1. You experienced a loss. Nonetheless, the fund manager took some positions during the year that had gains and produced dividends. You are liable for your share of those gains, even though you lost money on the fund.

Soft-dollar costs: Some mutual fund companies have third-party arrangements with brokerage firms that actually place the buys and sells for them. They make those transactions above market cost, in exchange perhaps for research that they

---

4 Ty A. Bernicke, "The Real Cost of Owning a Mutual Fund," *Forbes* (April 4, 2011), http://www.forbes.com/2011/04/04/real-cost-mutual-fund-taxes-fees-retirement-bernicke.html.

provide to the mutual fund management teams. In essence, that means you are paying above-market transaction costs for an arrangement behind the scenes.

Market-impact cost: Most funds have billions of dollars that they are required to invest somewhere. There are only so many securities available. So when the fund buys and sells securities, often the sheer volume can move the price of that security. Because funds try to avoid this, they can only buy or sell so much of one security at a time. In part, this is why we compare mutual funds to a huge, slowly turning wheel. Sometimes it can take months for a fund to become fully invested or divested from a particular security, not allowing them to be as reactive as might be necessary to get into or out of positions. It's because of the massive amounts of money they have to invest that mutual funds are not always as efficient or effective as other investment solutions.

TIP OF THE ICEBERG

None of those costs that we just described are transparent. The only cost that's transparent are the fees that they disclose in the prospectus, such as the marketing or distribution fee that you pay at the close of each market day. Nonetheless, despite what you are shown, you are paying all those other expenses. Few people understand that. In fact, few advisors know about all the hidden costs.

Mutual funds are well marketed and therefore quite familiar to the public. The marketers try to get the consumers to focus on what they think they are paying in costs. Mutual funds typically are sold as A, B, or C shares. For example, an A share would have a front-end commission of 3 to 5 percent, depending on the fund family, type of fund and how much you invest. That makes it relatively easy to identify the cost to invest in the fund: on a $100 investment with a 5 percent sales load, you would see $95 actually invested. The $5 might seem pretty expensive. Then, once you invest that money, who manages the shares? A lot of funds have worked to reduce the management fees, so people will look at the prospectus and see a management fee of 0.5 percent, which might seem reasonable.

But that's just the tip of the iceberg. The expense that people don't know about lies in the construction of the mutual fund. A small-cap or mid-cap fund manager, for example, will be buying two thousand to three thousand positions. If you were making that many trades in a self-directed brokerage account, you would be paying a significant cost to build that portfolio. And yet that is exactly what happens inside mutual funds. You're not just paying the front-end commissions and management fee. You must consider the purchasing of every individual security within the portfolio. And you must consider the turnover ratio: How often are all those positions bought and sold throughout the year? That's where the major hidden expenses show up in the mutual fund portfolio. That might be three times higher than the management fee, and it's not transparent.

It's not that the mutual fund is trying to mislead: if you asked the fund manager what the turnover ratio would be, he or she would say that's hard to tell, it all depends on what is happening in the stock market in the next twelve months. You can't precisely anticipate those costs, but you can see what transactions were made in the last 12 months and add that cost to all other fees that we outlined to get a sense of the total cost of investing in that mutual fund, including what is happening behind the scenes

OVERLAP AND HANDCUFFS

People often will own five, ten, or fifteen mutual funds within their portfolio. Those funds could include thousands of securities, with a lot of overlap. After all, the mutual fund companies are not about to share information on what they are buying and selling. One mutual fund in your portfolio might be buying AT&T stock and another might be selling it—and you are paying transaction costs both ways. The lack of communication between management teams leads to excess transactional expenses in your overall portfolio.

Another big risk to the mutual fund portfolio is that the manager is more or less handcuffed. Let's say you are buying a mutual fund that deals at all times in large-cap stocks. What happens to that mutual fund if large caps are going south, as happened in 2008–09? The fund still has to keep buying that particular variety of stocks regardless of market conditions. That is what the fund prospectus requires the manager to do.

What that underscores is that the construction of the mutual fund can limit the ability to truly manage the portfolio, resulting in a lack of diversification. In the planning process, we evaluate your mutual funds and the fees within them. We use a third-party software system to highlight hidden fees. We can see how the fees compare to the industry average of 3 or 4 percent. Not all funds have a high cost, but it is not uncommon to see fees at 4 or 5 percent. We have seen them as high as 8 percent. If you have one like that, you probably will want to dump it right away. You probably should get rid of the ones at 4 or 5 percent as well. You won't know what to do, though, unless you can identify the hidden costs.

INSTITUTIONAL TRANSPARENCY

We conduct a portfolio analysis to identify the specific costs within each of your mutual funds, so that you can decide whether they are acceptable. As a consumer, you need a clear picture of what you pay for services received. If you have a

$500,000 portfolio, and you're paying 3 percent on that investment, that's $15,000 a year. In ten years, that's $150,000 of investment expenses. If you can reduce that to any degree, you put money in your pocket—as well as the additional amount you can make by putting those savings to work for you.

Our advisory fees are always transparent to our clients. We put them in writing and discuss them, and we all sign off on them. Whenever you invest money in equities or bonds or any type of market-driven investment, there always will be some expenses. The question is how much are they, and can you see them all?

As a fiduciary firm, we use a transparent model of institutional investing. This is the type of investing employed by large pension plans, foundations, and endowments—some of the biggest pools of money out there. The advisory fee and transactional costs must be fully disclosed and transparent. Institutional pricing is among the lowest in the industry. At a penny a share, you would pay a dollar if you bought a hundred shares of IBM, or $1.36 if you sold 136 shares. You would see that cost right on the statement.

TO BE TRULY DIVERSIFIED

The institutional approach also allows us to truly create a diversified portfolio, custom-built around your risk tolerance. It is up to the institutional management team to create a diversified portfolio that is not bound by a prospectus. With this approach, the client becomes the prospectus. For example, if the aim is to achieve a 5 percent return, there is no prospectus saying we have to use large-cap companies. We might use international companies. We might use bonds, treasuries, or small-cap. We can use whatever investment is out there to seek that 5 percent return with an acceptable amount of risk.

By getting rid of that prospectus, we can truly build a diversified portfolio based on risk tolerance and investment objectives. Some investments might seek the 5 percent while others focus on companies known to do well in inflationary times. Others might hedge commodities. The risk tolerance is specific to each portfolio and what you are trying to accomplish. The buying and selling is not based upon what some prospectus requires.

This type of institutional portfolio also can promote tax efficiency. A mutual fund manager doesn't generally have as much flexibility in mitigating the impact of taxation in the portfolio. A custom portfolio, however, can be designed to minimize the amount of capital gains that are incurred. Such tax strategies can play a significant role in adding to your net worth.

We're not saying that mutual funds are all bad. If you are twenty or thirty years old and are just trying to stockpile as much money as you can in a 401(k) plan, mutual funds can get the job done. You will not need that money for a long time, so you can ride out the ups and downs of the market. But as you near retirement, you need to maximize the efficiencies of your investment. At that stage of life, mutual funds are normally not the best place to invest due to their higher expenses, inefficient construction, and inability to be proactive and reactive in the management of resources.

CHAPTER 8

HEALTH MATTERS

At some point during their lives, 70 percent of people who are now turning age sixty-five can expect to need some form of long-term care, according to statistics from the US Department of Health and Human Services. As people live increasingly longer, they naturally become more vulnerable to the frailties of old age, despite major advances in health care. It's little wonder that some of the more common questions that we hear as we help people build their retirement plans are about how they can protect themselves from the high costs of that care.

As the population ages, facilities are rapidly filling up, and long-term care costs are skyrocketing. Many retirees worry that their life savings could evaporate if they need to enter a long-term care facility for an extended stay. The risk is quite real, and so the question becomes how do we go about covering it.

There are three main ways to do so: by purchasing long-term care insurance, by self-insuring, or by purchasing life insurance or annuities with long-term care supplements.

LONG-TERM CARE INSURANCE

A traditional approach is to purchase an insurance policy specifically designed to cover the various risks associated with long-term care. Overall, these policies provide the most comprehensive coverage of the three options.

The long-term care insurance market has changed substantially over the last five to ten years. Premiums have increased at the same time that the policies have become less generous in their coverage. We have seen a trend in the industry in which insurance companies have been requiring a higher premium to maintain coverage. Retirees who have been paying a set premium for years find themselves forced to decide whether to just drop their policy or find money in their budget to meet the higher cost. Some have abandoned their coverage when they are most susceptible to needing it.

SELF-INSURING

Another option is to self-insure, meaning you decide to simply use resources that you have accumulated to pay those high costs in the event that you should need long-term care. You might also use trust strategies to protect some of your assets.

This can be an expensive proposition. In Iowa, the cost of a stay in a typical long-term care facility is about $5,500 a month. That means you would be looking at an annual expense of $60,000 to $70,000, although we have seen facilities with costs as high as $18,000 a month. You can imagine the type of portfolio that you would need to pay for a stay of just five years. At $60,000 a year, that would be $300,000. If you were going the fully self-insured route, we would have to identify within the portfolio for a married couple somewhere between $600,000 to $800,000 and designate that portion to pay for long-term care.

Of course, many of the expenses of living outside of the facility would no longer exist. In that way, self-insurance might not be as onerous as it might seem to some people. Nonetheless, this is an option that you likely will consider only if you have a high level of wealth. It's out of reach for most.

Those who are self-insuring need to be willing to accept Medicaid assistance if they get to the point where their resources do run out. Once you no longer can pay on your own, you become eligible for Title 19 and the state helps to support your long-term care needs.

Often, people who lack the resources to self-insure and who have no other form of coverage will be depending upon Medicaid assistance from the beginning if they need long-term care. Others who do have resources will employ a strategy in which they move some of those assets into a trust or gift them to family members. This must be done long before you need the care, however, because most states engage a five-year look back provision to check for any such sheltering of assets. Any resources still held in your name, as well as any assets that you moved within those five years, must be spent down before you will be eligible for assistance.

SUPPLEMENTAL APPROACH

The third strategy for obtaining long-term care coverage is to purchase a life insurance policy or annuity that includes long-term care benefits. Many people are reluctant to pay the high premium costs for a traditional long-term care policy that they might never need to use. Nor do they want to allocate such a large sum within their portfolio to self-insure when that money can be put to other uses. They think, perhaps, of a friend who paid a fortune in premiums, only to die of a heart attack on the golf course.

The supplemental approach therefore uses investment strategies with features that can offset some of the costs of long-term care if it's needed. For example, you might have a $100,000 universal life policy that would pay that much as a death benefit to your survivors but which would also advance you 20 percent of that benefit per year for up to 5 years if a doctor certified that you needed assistance with any two of the six "activities of daily living": eating, bathing, dressing, toileting, transferring, and continence. If you never need long-term care, you are not paying premiums to no avail: you still have the benefit of the permanent life insurance policy or of the annuity.

You likely would need more than $20,000 a year to pay for all of your long-term care, so you can purchase a policy that is appropriate to supplement your needs. The provisions vary widely in the extent of your long-term care risk that they will cover. You would also be supplementing some of those expenses through other savings and investments.

In other words, you effectively are reducing the amount that you would need to set aside for self-insurance. This is a combination approach in which you are making a calculated decision on how much of the risk you wish to transfer, with the advantage that if you never need long-term care you will still have the benefit of the permanent life insurance policy or of the annuity. Those premiums will count for something.

MEDICARE AND MORE

Health-care costs in general will be rising as you get older. The cost of medical care and products has been growing at a pace far greater than the ordinary inflation rate, and older people inevitably will require more and more of those goods and services. The combination of rising costs and rising needs can punch a hole in a family budget.

One important consideration is that if you retire before age sixty-five, when Medicare kicks in, you will experience a gap in medical coverage. Until then, you would need to use either a personal health insurance plan or perhaps a COBRA strategy from the group plan at your former employer.

At age sixty-five, you should file for what is known as Part A of Medicare or you may face a 10 percent permanent penalty. Many people will file for Part B at the same time, especially if they are not covered under a group health plan. Often, people with a group health plan will hold off on filing for Part B. When you turn sixty-six, you will be paying a Part B premium if you're not covered by a group plan.. It will come out of your Social Security check, and it will be based upon your wages in the previous two years. The standard premium currently is $121.80 per month, but this total depends on the previous two years of your income. If you were making more than $214,000, for example, you might have to pay $209 for that Part B premium. With advance planning strategies, you might be able to keep that premium lower as you transition into retirement. For additional information on Medicare costs, go to medicare.gov.

A lot of people consider retiring at sixty-two but decide to wait because they feel they cannot afford the additional $800 to $1200 a month that they might need to pay to continue their health insurance until they are eligible for Medicare coverage. What they may not realize is that those additional years of high wages could increase their Part B premiums at the beginning of their retirement. When they give up W2 wages and the record falls off in a couple years, they will return to normal Part B rates.

As you can see, you have much to consider and balance when making these decisions. All those parts and supplements and deadlines can get confusing, and due to legislative changes the answers to questions are constantly changing. You will do well to seek professional guidance. To make sure that our clients get the best and latest information, we have partners who are full-time health-care specialists with the expertise to make sure these risks are covered appropriately and efficiently.

CHAPTER 9

REPLACING THE PAYCHECK

It can be a daunting prospect to switch from the sustainable and dependable income of your working years to what might seem a far less-certain scenario in retirement. In fact, it requires a fundamental shift in mind-set.

So much is different now, and you will be dealing with these changes throughout your retirement years. For one thing, your investments must account for inflation. Yes, your Social Security benefit has cost-of-living adjustments, but historically they have averaged less than the inflation rate. It will be up to you or your financial planner to design a portfolio that rises to the challenge.

BUCKETS OF MONEY

To address that and other issues, we use a "bucket" strategy for retirement income planning. Think of these as containers for your money that you can set aside for separate purposes, similar to the buckets that we described for tax planning. You could have a variety of buckets, but there are three main ones. Those are the foundation bucket, the growth bucket, and the dream bucket.

The primary objective of the foundation bucket is to provide money that is very conservatively invested and ideally would provide a guaranteed income. You want a secure and dependable investment that will suffer no losses, even in a market as dismal as 2008. The primary objectives in this bucket are safety and liquidity. You need to be able to access it at any time without penalty. In some markets these investments also will provide decent growth to beat or at least meet inflation, but that is not the main aim here. What you need here is a reliable income for both now and further down the road. This is the foundation of your portfolio.

The growth bucket will include investments that are able to provide a return that, in the long term, will build the portfolio and beat inflation. Liquidity is not the concern here, nor is the emphasis so much on safety. Since these are longer-term investments, they can be placed at somewhat greater risk in the market because they will have a chance to recover if the economy turns south.

The dream bucket is for investments that you are making toward accomplishing something important to you—perhaps an Alaskan cruise or a European vacation. This is for the goals that get you excited, that give you a reason to get up and keep your mind and body active. The manner in which your dollars are invested in this bucket will depend on your time horizon for those particular dreams. If they are in the distant future, you can utilize more investment risk. If the dream will soon be at your doorstep, you will not want to run much risk with this money.

Within these buckets, you might have others—how many will depend largely on your resources and your goals. Every few years you can give yourself a raise, turning on a spigot from whichever bucket is most appropriate at the time. What you must *not* do is take an income from money that has depreciated. Your current income bucket needs to be sufficient to support you for six to twelve months so that you will not be tempted to dip into those longer-term assets when they are down. That way you will not be risking the devastation that the sequence of returns could inflict.

These buckets are a concrete way of thinking about the concept of asset allocation. You will not necessarily have several separate investment accounts, but you certainly will have financial vehicles that serve separate purposes in your portfolio. The buckets are a way of thinking about what you are trying to accomplish with a particular portion of your money. Within your portfolio, you will be investing in various ways, some of which function as the foundation bucket, some as the growth bucket, and some as the dream bucket.

Each financial product has its place, according to its purpose, and should be used appropriately. What works well in one bucket might serve poorly in another. When positioned properly in your portfolio, they will be able to function as they were designed for your short-term, mid-term, or long-term planning.

This approach to income planning helps you to keep in check the emotions that can be as volatile as the marketplace. If you have money in the market, you can be virtually assured that at some point its value will be falling, to a greater or lesser extent. When you see a portion of your life savings draining away, it's a less-than-pleasant ride. Still, you are likely to come through unscathed if you keep the plan in mind and focus on whether you are on track toward the goals that you have set for your retirement. That is the perspective and assurance that you can gain from a well-crafted financial plan, regularly updated with the guidance of a professional advisor.

THE THREE WORLDS OF MONEY

When we teach adult education classes, we often ask people for examples of where they can invest money. And we get a variety of responses, the most common of which are stocks and bonds, mutual funds, certificates of deposit, exchange-traded funds, real estate investment trusts, and annuities.

Once the class has produced a sufficiently long list, we categorize those investments. We explain that there are three worlds of money. One is money in the market, which is the Wall Street world. This is the world of risk and includes investments that can go up and that can go down.

Another is the banking world, which includes CDs, savings accounts, and money market accounts—investments where the principal is protected. The investment is guaranteed not to lose value.

People are less familiar with the third world of money. These are investments that take a hybrid approach, seeking to combine the best of the banking world with the best of the Wall Street world.

Most people understand that diversification is a crucial concept, but what does that really mean? It means that you need money in each of those three worlds. Not only must all three worlds be represented in your portfolio, but each world, itself, also needs to be diversified.

Most people are not familiar with these types of strategies. They long have focused on the at-risk world of Wall Street, and most of their portfolio has been designed that way. A hybrid approach in their safety bucket actually can tap into the upside potential of the market without the downside risk.

To illustrate, suppose you were investing $100,000 starting in the high-flying market year of 1998. If you invested that amount in the world of Wall Street, getting the return of the S&P 500 index, your money would have grown to $120,000 that year. With a hybrid approach, you only would have had $115,000. That's because you gave up some of the potential gain to hedge against the possibility of loss.

HYBRID APPROACH

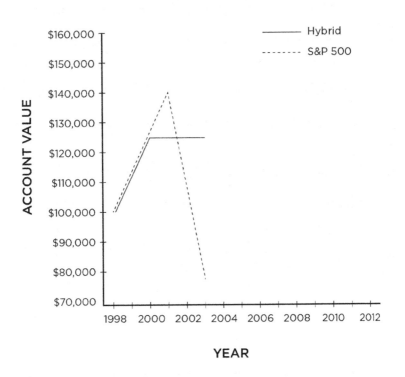

The next year, you would have had $136,000 in the at-risk account and $125,000 in the hybrid account. Then came the terrible period of 2000 to 2002. If all of that $100,000 was in the Wall Street bucket, you would have ended up with

$78,000. In the hybrid bucket, you would have stayed steady at $125,000.

As you can clearly see, to have that upside potential without the downside risk can be highly advantageous to your portfolio. Yes, you will be limited on some of the gains, but you will be protecting yourself from losses. This can be a powerful strategy in your retirement planning.

A REASONABLE WITHDRAWAL RATE

You need to be cognizant of the percentage of your portfolio that you are taking out as income from your investable assets. The financial media and many planners will often suggest a 4 percent withdrawal strategy, but such a strategy calls for caution.

The rationale behind the strategy is based on the belief that long-term market averages conservatively will allow such a withdrawal. However, that is presuming interest rates that are at average levels. Recently, we have not been close to such levels. In this type of economic environment, withdrawing at that rate from a fluctuating account can eventually make a mess of your portfolio, particularly if the sequence of returns, as we explained earlier, does not fall in your favor.

Let's say you have a $500,000 portfolio and your goal is to withdraw 4 percent for a $20,000 supplement to your income. If your earnings on that portfolio are 4 percent or better, that should work fine. But suppose you encounter a year like 2008 and you lose 30 percent of your nest egg. You now have a $350,000 portfolio. Now, if you withdraw your 4 percent, you will only realize a $14,000 income. If you are depending on that $20,000 and take that much out anyway, your withdrawal rate will now be 5.7 percent.

In effect, you will be kicking your portfolio when it's already down. Even if you choose not to deliver that kick, you will need a prodigious return the next year (about 50 percent) just to get back to your original $500,000. Clearly, you face a dilemma, and it could persist for the rest of your retirement. Either you will need to immediately curtail your lifestyle, or you will be running out of money, which will curtail it even more.

That is why you need to carefully monitor the percentage of withdrawal from your portfolio. This risk highlights the importance of the foundational bucket that we described earlier in this chapter. By tapping that bucket instead of your market investments, you can avoid doing such damage to your portfolio. The money that you have subjected to risk can be left alone to recover from a market plunge.

INVESTMENT AND SPENDING RISK

Investment risk is one of the two main threats that could jeopardize a successful outcome for the financial plans that we develop for our clients. If a portfolio loses 30 or 40 percent, it will severely diminish retirement ambitions. When we begin working with clients, we almost always find that they have been taking on far too much investment risk based on their resources and their goals. We address that risk immediately.

The other major risk involves their living expenses. We look to see whether they are spending too much currently or whether they are running the risk of doing so later. Most people we meet actually do a good job of managing current expenses. The main problem that we find is that they are not accounting for unforeseen events, particularly in the health arena, that could greatly increase their expenses and deplete their retirement resources much faster than anticipated.

When we bring up the importance of the budgeting process, some people take it quite seriously. They examine the last twelve months of their checking account and determine what they actually spent—and for most, it's significantly higher than they had realized. Then we take a look at the resources that they have acquired, and based on a few conservative assumptions, we can determine how much they reasonably can afford to spend and what their retirement will look like in twenty years if they maintain that level of spending. We then find out whether they feel comfortable with that assessment.

A lot of people have only a general idea of their expenses. They don't examine the line items. They have long figured that if the expenses start to mount, they can just work some more overtime or take on an extra project at work to make up for any shortfalls. Because they are not used to budgeting, they don't really know how to answer when we ask them what their budget includes. The look on their faces tells us that this is not a monthly exercise for them.

In truth, it's not that important for the planning process that we know every single line item, such as how much they spend on cable or their weekly tab at the grocery store. What is more critical is the overall amount that they have been spending, month in and month out.

Let's say you use credit cards as your main means of buying goods and services. Take a look at how much you spent each month in the past year; was it $5,000? $4,000? If you look at a whole year, you will start to see the typical amount you tend to spend in a month. Some months will be more, and some will be less. You're looking for an average so that you get a true picture of your monthly income needs in retirement.

It's an important step in devising your overall financial plan for retirement. If you head into retirement thinking that you are only going to be spending $3,000 a month, and it turns out to be $5,000 a month, eventually you are likely to find yourself looking for a part-time job. We have seen numerous cases where people who did not adequately project their fixed expenses end up back in the workforce several years after leaving it.

These are distinct risks, and we can help to prevent them through our early evaluation of investment and spending. In our risk analysis, we look at how much risk you are currently taking and how much you need to take. Then we set up the investments to meet your established goals, also keeping in mind your tolerance for risk.

Understand that the scenario is likely to change during your retirement years. Today's workable financial plan might need to be significantly different in a year. Your financial plan, including your investment, legacy, and income strategies, needs to be flexible enough to change as life changes.

CHAPTER 10

PRESERVING YOUR LEGACY

We recently met with a gentleman whose wife had passed away three months previously. She had two tax-deferred accounts in her name. One was an IRA, and the other was a 401(k) plan. Together, they totaled just over $1 million.

Unfortunately, those accounts had been incorrectly coded for the beneficiary, and so for three months he had been fighting to gain access to the plans. He would have been readily able to move that money into his own IRA if the accounts had been appropriately titled..

Instead, he had to incur the cost and hassle of probate. In the state of Iowa, it typically costs about 4 percent of the value of assets to move them through probate. On a $1 million portfolio, that amounts to about $40,000. That is the cost that he faced in fighting for access to accounts that so easily could have been transferred with a simple signature prior to his wife's death. In Iowa it takes at least six months, and often more than a year, to get through probate and collect the inheritance. Meanwhile, the time-consuming process was exposing the portfolio to the potential of claims from creditors.

You might call that a mess. None of that, however, was his biggest issue. The probate process meant that those assets no longer would be tax-deferred when he received them. He would have $1 million subject to taxation, and that would put him in the highest marginal tax bracket. The IRS at times makes exceptions in situations such as his, but that involves paying the costs of attorneys and further delays—with no guarantees.

All of this was the consequence of one slip-up, the mistitling of the accounts. All they would have had to do was appropriately prepare the documents, and the money would have been his, free and clear, within his IRA.

Had he begun working with us sooner, this all would have been avoided. As part of our planning process, we do a review to make sure that our clients' accounts have been properly titled, both for ownership and for beneficiary. This is easy to do while the account owner is alive. It's highly difficult, if it's possible at all, for the survivors to fix that problem once the owner has passed on. And they will need to contend with the tax situation—which can be the biggest mess of all.

CUTTING THROUGH THE CONFUSION

When we talk about preserving a legacy, a lot of people get confused because they have heard so much of the legal jargon that gets wrapped around these strategies. Cutting through that confusion is imperative if we are to establish an effective and appropriate legacy plan to maximize resources not only while you are alive but also after you have passed on.

Your money is a measure of your hard work and your talents, represented after all those years as a balance on a statement. That is one reflection of your accomplishments, but the real power of your legacy will be in making sure that your life has added up to something of significance for the world.

We recently attended a discussion at a large hospital in our community on the power of advanced legacy planning techniques to do good in the world. If you have money sitting in a bank that you will not be needing, or if you are required to take distributions from a retirement plan that you will not be spending, there are strategies that can multiply those moneys for the benefit of causes and institutions that are meaningful to you.

Most people want to give back in some way. They want to make the world a better place. A variety of powerful strategies can fulfill those wishes. We can set up trusts and use provisions of the tax code to maximize resources for the greater good while also streamlining families' estate planning.

It's frequently said that if you fail to plan, you can plan on failing. It's so oft-repeated because it so often holds true. We have seen families destroyed by not having any type of plan. It's left to the brother-in-law or sister-in-law or siblings to try to figure out where the money should go. The lack of planning can be highly disruptive to loved ones' lives.

If you don't have a plan, the government *certainly* will have one for you. It stands ready to claim a major share of your legacy and distribute it in the manner it sees fit. To prevent that, you need a vision. You should be giving a lot of thought to where and how you wish to direct the proceeds of your life's work.

WILLS AND TRUSTS

A will gives your heirs specific legal instructions on where you want your property and remaining assets to go when you are gone. However, it still must go through probate. In Iowa, an estate is "probatable" if it's above $25,000. Again, the cost can be around 4 percent of the estate's value, and it could be many months before your beneficiaries can receive those assets.

Anything that goes through probate becomes public information. The system is designed that way so that creditors can come in to lay a claim. As your heirs sort through the legalities of those claims, the probate time can get considerably longer.

If you set up a *revocable trust*, however, the assets that pass through the trust will not be subjected to probate. They can go almost immediately to the beneficiaries, avoiding the probate costs. Another advantage is that assets going through a trust do not become public information.

It costs more to set up a trust than it costs to set up a will. It can be well worth it, though, because the trust can save your estate a significant amount of money by shielding it from all of the probate costs. In Iowa, the average cost to set up a trust is about $3,000, depending upon its complexity. The average cost to set up a will is probably $250 or $300. Often, the best strategy is to have both a will and a trust. There are many reasons why you might want both. A last will can do different things that a trust cannot, for example, provide guardianship instructions for minor children, forgive debts, and handle any property that isn't included in the trust document.

You cannot take shortcuts with those beneficiary designations; they must be set up correctly. It might be tempting to think, *This is complicated, so I'll just name my son as a joint owner on my account, and he'll take care of it.* Taking such estate planning shortcuts can potentially be quite risky, and you need to think about the consequences. Is it possible that your son could get divorced? There goes half of that account balance. What if he loses a lawsuit?

With a trust, you can exercise controls over payouts—who gets the money and when and under what circumstances. That might seem a good reason to establish a trust as beneficiary for an IRA or 401(k) plan, but be very careful in doing so. This calls for precise wording with the guidance of a qualified estate-planning attorney who specializes in such matters. Generally speaking, designating a trust as the primary beneficiary doesn't make sense—because of tax considerations. As we pointed out earlier, the trust cannot ordinarily exercise the stretch provision that is available with IRAs and some 401(k)s, and therefore it would be required to liquidate the total value of the retirement plan within five years. That could expose most of that income to taxation at the 35 percent trust rate. Setting something like this up efficiently requires that specific language be incorporated into the trust. Most of the time, if the trust is to be a beneficiary, it should be as a contingent—not as the primary.

GIVING BACK

When people see libraries and hospitals and other institutions named after a prominent family, they think of how much wealth must be involved for anyone to be able to contribute at such a grand level. And certainly, those are examples of how great affluence can turn to great beneficence.

All around us, however, is the evidence of more modest and yet meaningful giving: a playground at a zoo, a bench in a city park, a brick in a sidewalk that bears the name of an individual or couple or family who cared enough to donate to a worthy cause. Those are not necessarily the contributions from multimillion-dollar estates. Much of the charitable work in our nation comes from people of lesser means who did a bit of planning and found ways to make a difference.

Giving back to your community is not so much about how *much* money you have as it is about your desire to *maximize* whatever resources are available to you. Perhaps you are grateful for a comfortable lifestyle and do not really need those regular distributions that you are required to take from your retirement plan. You might decide to donate that money to charity rather than see much of it go to taxes. Or you might put the money into a life insurance policy and structure the beneficiary so that someday children might play at a park that you helped to build. You need not command millions to do your part in changing the world. You can do it bit by bit, brick by brick.

Any one of these many strategies might be the best ones to enhance your legacy. A competent team on your side can help you determine which methods would be most effective for you and your family. That team should include special-ists in retirement planning, estate planning, and accounting. As retirement planners, our role is to help bring those minds together and coordinate them to provide the best service possible for our clients. An effective estate plan needs to be a collaborative effort involving those who know how to make it work most efficiently for the benefit of all.

TO A PROSPEROUS FUTURE

Your retirement plan is pivotal in helping you to make confident decisions that will increase the probability of many successful years ahead. We are in a new era of retirement planning. Thirty or forty years ago, people typically left the workforce with a healthy pension and a Social Security check that they could count on for the rest of their lives. They could enjoy a comfortable retirement with a lot less planning.

Back then, the primary planning objective was to make sure that you worked at the same company for most of your career so that you could get that generous pension. No more. The once ubiquitous pensions are rapidly disappearing, and we are likely to see continuing abridgments to the Social Security system. In short, retirees have become increasingly dependent upon whatever resources they have been able to accumulate during their working lives. That has made effective planning strategies imperative.

You can be certain that the government has a plan. That plan is to take away as much of your resources as possible to sustain what the government is trying to accomplish. That is why you need to counter with your own plan to make sure that you maintain as much control as possible over those resources.

Imagine a world where you have that control. Imagine a world where you have confidence that the decisions you are making will benefit you, your loved ones, and your community—both now and into the decades ahead. You worked hard to save and accumulate those resources. Now you deserve to make the most of them.

Suppose that one fine morning we were to stuff a million dollars into a suitcase and tell you that we had placed it on a doorstep somewhere in your city—and that it would be yours to keep if you could find it before the sun went down. You might protest that such a task would be next to impossible. But suppose we gave you a map, with X marks the spot, or the GPS coordinates for where you could find that treasure. You no doubt would scurry out to lay claim to your reward.

That's what it's like to map out the path to a successful retirement. If you head out with no sense of direction and no vision of where you are going, hoping things just work out, it will be next to impossible to get very far without feeling frustrated and disappointed. With reliable guidance, however, you can proceed with confidence and clarity to the destination of your dreams.

OUR MISSION STATEMENT:

Weiss-Merkle Financial is dedicated to providing the financial expertise you need and the retirement experience you deserve. Through life-long relationships, we work with you to create a comprehensive plan so you can achieve the retirement of your dreams.

It is our vision, through education and guidance, to empower everyone to retire with confidence and to enjoy financial freedom.

- -

You can contact Weiss-Merkle Financial
by calling us at **515-278-4110**
or emailing **info@weissmerklefinancial.com**.
You can also visit our website at
www.weissmerklefinancial.com
and watch our weekly TV show on ABC 5
every Sunday at 10:30 AM.

- -

CPSIA information can be obtained
at www.ICGtesting.com
Printed in the USA
BVOW06s1417150217
476305BV00015B/429/P

9 781599 327174